The Developing Countries and the World Economic Order

The Developing Countries and the World Economic Order

Lars Anell and Birgitta Nygren
The Swedish Secretariat for Future Studies

METHUEN
LONDON AND NEW YORK

5862

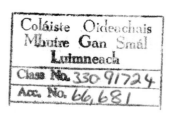
First published in Great Britain in 1980 by
Frances Pinter (Publishers) Limited
5 Dryden Street, London WC2E 9NW

First published as a University Paperback in 1980 by
Methuen & Co. Ltd
11 New Fetter Lane, London EC4P 4EE
Reprinted 1982

University Paperback edition published in the
United States of America by
Methuen & Co.
in association with Methuen, Inc.
733 Third Avenue, New York, NY 10017

© 1980 Lars Anell and Birgitta Nygren

Printed in Great Britain by
J. W. Arrowsmith Ltd, Bristol

ISBN 0 416 74630 6

CONTENTS

PREFACE

This book is part of an attempt by the Swedish Secretariat for Futures Studies to stimulate the debate on the NIEO. It is written by Lars Anell (chaps. 2, 4 and 5) and Birgitta Nygren (chap. 3). Lars Anell was on leave of absence from his post as head of the Planning Department in the Foreign Ministry's Office for International Development Cooperation. Birgitta Nygren was earlier engaged in the Federation of Swedish Industries and the United Nations Industrial Development Organization, UNIDO.

The introductory chapter of the report gives an overview of some of the points of departure and central questions to be dealt with.

The first chapters contain a relatively detailed account of the background to the demands of developing countries for a new international economic order. A survey of the economic development up to the Second World War and of the colonial heritage of the developing countries is followed by an account of the way in which the postwar world order came into being. Chapter 3 provides an account of the cooperation between the developing countries and the background to the resolutions passed at, among others, the Sixth and Seventh Special Sessions of the UN General Assembly. The texts of the declaration and the programme of action for the establishment of a New International Economic Order (NIEO) adopted by the UN General Assembly in May 1974 are reproduced in Appendix 1.

The rest of the book is of an analytical and commentatory nature. Chapter 4 contains a critical analysis of some of the central NIEO demands. Chapter 5 is primarily an attempt to outline a new perspective on the NIEO programme, to indicate some of the points of departure for an equitable world order and to suggest some possible ways in which the developing countries could secure for themselves a larger share of the world's resources. A major theme of the report is that important changes in the world order take place irrespective of the recommendations adopted at international conferences.

It is impossible to name all the people who have contributed to this report with ideas and comments. The authors do, however, wish to express particular gratitude to Carl Hamilton, Lars Ingelstam, Sverker Jonsson, Ola Johansson, Lennart Klackenberg and Staffan Sohlman and, for help in typing it, to Agneta Frögren, Margareta Granäs and Anita Klintsell-Pettersson.

Stockholm, November 1979

Lars Ingelstam
Director
Secretariat for Futures Studies

INTRODUCTION

In the spring of 1974 the UN General Assembly gathered for its Sixth Special Session. The developing countries had asked for this session to be convened; and they set the tone of the proceedings.

After working for almost a month the delegates were able to produce a long list of principles and proposals concentrated into a declaration and a programme of action. The heading indicated that the recommendations adopted were aimed to show how a *New International Economic Order* (NIEO) should be established.

The concept of the New International Economic Order or world order was rapidly introduced into debates on the developing countries. Many developed countries adopted a clearly positive attitude to NIEO. But is that because the concept of NIEO has been reduced to a slogan that each particular group interprets in the light of its own wishful thinking? People often talk about *the* new world order, but too little has been said about the form this new order will take. What is an international order in any case? How does it function and who or what can guarantee that the order is maintained?

These are some of the questions that we shall endeavour to answer in this book. Our intention is simply to attempt to provide a better framework for the debate.

Another purpose is to examine critically the most important of the demands presented by the developing countries. The question that has to be answered is simply whether the proposals of the developing countries would lead to a more even distribution of the resources between the earth's inhabitants, which must be the central aim. In any case, this is our starting point when we analyse the demands that have been put forward.

There are also grounds for considering whether the fact that the debate and the negotiations are directed towards establishing a NIEO may not have some less desirable effects. In conclusion we shall endeavour to indicate some of the fundamental requirements that must be satisfied by an *equitable* economic world order.

The realisation of how difficult these problems are compels us to reiterate that this book is intended to stimulate debate as well as to inform. For that reason some free speculation and loose hypotheses will be permitted. A few open doors will undoubtedly be forced — if that is not an impossible feat — while we proceed towards more formidable obstacles. We have also chosen in some cases to ignore the fact that politics is the art of the possible.

The original intention was to include in this publication a brief account of the background to the events that took place during 1973-74 and led up to the Sixth Special Session of the UN General Assembly. During the course of our work, however, we found that the economic situation and demands of the developing countries cannot be understood without a fairly clear description of how the present world order has evolved. That is the reason for the length of the introductory chapter on the historical background. We can only hope that the readers will agree with our assessment.

LIST OF TABLES

1 HISTORICAL BACKGROUND

The existing world order can be explained in several ways. It may be seen as the result of a long historical process — the industrial revolution, which began in Great Britain at the end of the eighteenth century, spread to the European continent and the United States and, in the second half of the nineteenth century, reached most parts of Europe, Japan and the 'peripheral' countries of Scandinavia. It may also be seen as the result of the decisions taken by the allied powers, led by the United States, during and immediately after the Second World War.

But these two explanations are basically the same. The process of economic development gave the major industrial countries a decisive influence over the world economy. The two world wars strengthened the military and economic position of the United States.

TOWARDS AN INTERNATIONAL ECONOMY

An international world economy began to emerge soon after the end of the Napoleonic wars in Europe. Industrialisation had already gathered momentum in Great Britain. The international consequences of this followed during the nineteenth century.

Throughout the hundred years which ended in 1913 world trade and the international transfers of capital increased far more quickly than population and production. At the beginning of the nineteenth century only about 3 per cent of production was circulated through international trade. By 1913 world trade was equivalent to about a third of the total world output (1).

The reasons for this development are principally connected with the fact that industrialism spread to more and more countries. Technological development was export-oriented (2) — cheap machine-made articles replaced handicraft products or production for household use. The decline in economic self-sufficiency led to large-scale investments in roads, canals and railways. The rapid growth of production caused a greater demand for raw materials. The demand for foodstuffs from the growing towns was met primarily by expanding domestic production, but in a few countries, of which the most important was Great Britain, there soon arose a substantial need to import foodstuffs (3). Higher real wages in industry led to an increased demand for tropical products such as coffee, tea, cocoa, tobacco and sugar.

There was also an ecological background to industrialism. An acute land shortage forced a growing proportion of the population to sell their labour in the towns. Capitalism is not just a system in which people can freely sell their labour power; another precondition, as the German sociologist Max Weber pointed out (4), is that they are forced to do so.

The removal of the obstacles to trade which occurred in the mid-nineteenth century never became particularly long-lasting or widespread — except in Great Britain. But the relative freedom that prevailed in the first part of the second half of the nineteenth century contributed to a growth of 270 per cent in the volume of world trade during the period 1850–1880. Economic depression and rising tariffs caused a slowing-down of the growth — to 170 per cent during the period 1880-1913 (5).

Technological conditions for the expansion of world trade were created by a rapid development of domestic and international communications. The total shipping tonnage of the world increased from 19 million tons in 1870 to 49 million in 1913, almost half of which consisted of steamships (6). The freight rates fell by 75 per cent during the period 1820–1850 (7) and by 70–90 per cent between the middle of the nineteenth century and the outbreak of the Great War. In 1840 there were 8,000 km of railways in the whole world, thirty years later 210,000 km and by the turn of the century nearly 800,000 km, of which roughly 100,000 km were in the developing countries of today (8).

The profits of the colonial trade and gains from higher production in agriculture generated a surplus for investments in industry and purchasing power for manufactured goods. Technological and organisational changes played an important part from an early date in both agriculture and industry (9). And the new technology spread, due, for one thing, to the fact that skilled workers were induced to emigrate from Great Britain. A witness before a British parliamentary committee estimated that 16,000 highly skilled workers moved to France during the two years 1822–23 alone (10).

The real national income rose in step with the gains from higher productivity in industry and agriculture during practically the whole of the nineteenth century. This was true not only of Western Europe, North America and Japan, but also of several regions exporting primary commodities. In the United States, and after 1850 also in Canada and Brazil, the annual growth of national income per inhabitant is estimated at about 1.5 per cent. In Latin America Argentina also experienced a rapid growth of income, particularly during the period after 1880. In Europe only Sweden and Denmark reached a rate of growth during the latter part of the nineteenth century comparable to that of North America. In most European countries the real per capita income rose by about 1 per cent. The increase for Australia was probably somewhat below 1.5 per cent a year and in the case of New Zealand it remained at around 0.5 per cent (11).

At an initial stage industrialisation probably gave rise to increased gaps in personal incomes. Gradually, however, real wages began to pick up and in the majority of the above-mentioned countries the wages component of the GNP rose markedly.

For the majority of countries in Asia, Africa and Latin America the statistics are unreliable and only qualified guesses are possible. For India there are calculations which indicate that the national income per capita grew by 0.4 per cent a year during the periods 1857–63 and 1896–1904 (12). For Japan there are very divergent calculations of the growth of output during 1880-1913. The growth was certainly very rapid, probably around 2 per cent (13). In other parts of Asia, Latin America and Africa the economic growth per inhabitant is calculated at 0.5 per cent or less per year (14). The variations around this average must in all likelihood have been considerable (15).

Great Britain was the dominant industrial nation by the mid-nineteenth century. Fairly soon after that, however, British industry began to lose ground, above all to its competitors in the United States and Germany. During the period 1870-1913 these two countries raised their combined share of world industrial production from 36 to 52 per cent while the share of Great Britain was reduced from 32 to 16 per cent. Sweden and Canada were among the industrial countries that developed most rapidly.

The volume of world trade grew, as we have said, far more rapidly than total output throughout the century before the Great War. Exports and international trade became more and more important for economic growth. In virtually all industrial countries the share of production that was exported increased very markedly. France may have been an exception to this rule (16).

The changing economic positions of the major industrial powers — as reflected in their changing share of world industrial production — had very small impact in the sphere of trade. Great Britain's share of world trade fell only from 15 per cent in 1876 to 14 per cent in 1913, while the country's share of world industrial output was more than halved. The rapid emergence of the United States as the world's leading industrial nation was not reflected at all in trade statistics before 1913. It is interesting that the primary commodity producing countries in Asia, Africa and Latin America during the period 1876-1913 more than maintained their share of world trade; in the case of Africa and Latin America the share clearly increased, while it diminished slightly in the case of Asia (17).

The distribution of world trade between primary commodities and manufactured products appears to have been relatively stable during the hundred years up to 1913. Throughout the

Table 1 Share of world trade for selected countries 1885 and
1913.

	Share of world exports		Share of world imports	
	1885	*1913*	*1885*	*1913*
	%	%	%	%
Great Britain	16.7	13.9	21.0	15.8
France	9.6	7.2	10.9	8.0
Germany	11.0	13.1	9.6	12.6
Sweden	1.1	1.2	1.2	1.1
Western Europe	54.4	50.0	59.5	56.4
United States	11.2	10.9	9.0	9.8

Source: Bunte & Jörberg, p. 24

period for which statistics are fairly reliable, the years 1876–
1913, trade in primary commodities constituted 63–64 per
cent of world trade (18). Of countries and colonies outside
Europe North America accounted for 35–40 per cent of the
total exports of primary commodities. The share of these
countries in the exports of manufactured products increased
from 1.5 per cent in 1876 to nearly 8 per cent in 1913, largely
due to the rapid growth of exports from Japan. Europe accounted
for as much as 94 per cent of world exports of manufactured
products in 1876, a share that had fallen to 82 per cent by 1913.

COLONIALISM

It may not have been quite as simple as the French premier
Jules Ferry put the matter when he stated in a book published
in 1890 that 'colonial policy is the daughter of industrialisation'
(19) but the century of industrialism also became that of
colonialism. And that there was a connection is undeniable
unless, as the Hungarian economist Tamás Szentes ironically
pointed out, one wishes to see 'the scramble of Africa' as the
result of 'the unfortunate coincidence, in a number of countries,
of people coming to power with the same propensity to run an
imperialist policy' (20).

It all began much earlier, as everyone knows. As early as
the fifteenth century Portuguese ships sailed first to the west
coast of Africa and then with Arab pilots (21) to Asia, and in

1493 the New World was divided with papal support between Spain and Portugal. The Spaniards and Portuguese arrived in the 'New World' with weapons and infectious diseases. They carried back to Europe gold, silver and the knowledge of how to cultivate potatoes, maize, tomatoes, chili pepper, groundnuts and manioc. While the population of large parts of Latin America was reduced to a tenth or a twentieth by epidemics of measles or small-pox, the foundations were laid in Western Europe for a money economy, rising population growth and a surplus-producing agriculture (22). During the seventeenth century the Dutch, English and French took over the command of the sea and founded their empires in Asia, the Caribbean and North America.

Towards the end of the eighteenth or at the beginning of the nineteenth century a contemporary observer might possibly have been able to forecast the dissolution of the colonial empires. The United States declared its independence in the same year as Adam Smith published *The Wealth of Nations* and asserted that colonies, at best, were unnecessary (23). The Latin American states, with few exceptions, became formally independent in the 1820s. There was no doubt that the regions colonised by European immigrants would eventually become independent. No European government except that of Russia had colonial acquisitions as a definite and consistent political goal during the period 1815–82 (24). The colonial annexations which took place were primarily aimed at reinforcing already acquired positions and spheres of interest. In several cases they were caused by the development within previously established colonies without the instigation of and with limited control from London and Paris.

Around 1870, therefore, the major part of Africa was still independent and unexplored. In West Africa the leading European trading nations were long satisfied with bases along the coast for the profitable triangular trade; factory products were exchanged in African coastal towns for slaves who were shipped to the plantations in the Caribbean and mainland America, from where tropical products were brought back to the factories of Europe. The total number of slaves transported under indescribable conditions from underpopulated Africa amounted to nearly ten million, about eight million of them during the period 1700–1870 (25).

The race for colonies took place during the last decades of the nineteenth century. Africa was divided up between Great Britain, France, Germany, Belgium, Portugal and Italy. The United States continued the expansion which had consisted in colonising her own continent by annexing Hawaii and conquering Cuba and the Philippines from Spain. Russia extended her Central Asian empire towards the east and the south. Japan gained control over Korea and Taiwan. China was forced to accept foreign control over foreign trade. In order to understand these developments one must distinguish between underlying motives and triggering factors.

In 1873 an economic depression began in Europe which was to last with short intervals up to the middle of the 1890s. Exports from Great Britain and France immediately decreased. From the beginning of the 1880s Germany's exports also decreased. Especially in France, which was to become the most aggressive colonising power, the export industry was hard hit. In Germany an increased interest in colonies coincided with a marked decline of export revenues in 1883–1885 (26).

Among professional economists it was a commonly held view that the economy of a country would eventually reach a stage of maturity. A surplus of investment capital would then lead to an inevitable fall in profits. This process could, however, be arrested by increased exports or investments abroad. The leading economist at that time, John Stuart Mill, had asserted in his standard work of economic theory *Principles of Political Economy* that 'the perpetual overflow of capital into colonies or foreign countries . . . has been for many years one of the principal causes by which the decline of profits in England has been arrested' (27).

It was not necessary, however, to solve the problem through new colonial acquisitions. It was sufficient to keep the door open for trade and investments. This was also the settled policy of Great Britain and Germany. These countries wished to avoid annexing new areas for as long as possible (28). The ultimate aim of nineteenth century imperialism was freedom for trade and capital. But the brief free trade epoch around the middle of the nineteenth century was rapidly coming to an end. In France protectionist tendencies increased. This brings us to the competition which triggered off the race for colonies.

During the 1880s France initiated a new and more aggressive colonial policy and the Belgian King Leopold II laid claim to large regions along the river Congo. Germany and Italy emerged as new colonial rivals. Great Britain occupied Egypt in 1882. The major powers became involved in intensive competition for the last blank spots on the map. All this led up to the Berlin Conference of 1884–85 which, in the words of the British historian D. K. Fieldhouse, 'by drawing up rules . . . declared the game in progress' (29).

When the race for colonies was actually under way, it gained a momentum which gradually increased and then pushed the process further. Business enterprises adapted themselves to the colonial trade. During the nineteenth century British cotton exports were increasingly directed towards developing countries, first Latin America and then the Far East (30). The demand for tropical raw materials increased. The economic interests of the upper class in the colonies grew. A retreat from the positions already won was impossible for the governments of prestige-ridden Europe.

All this provided opportunities for the colonial administrators themselves to push the colonial expansion further. Only a handful of members of the British government were informed of the developments which led to the Boer War (31). The annexation of Upper Burma is still more illuminating. It was carried out by a quick military action decided upon by the Governor General in India while the political scene in London was completely dominated by the Irish Home Rule crisis (32). The conquest of Lower Burma, which had occurred earlier, was also in the main the work of an expansionist and independent governor general. The official reason on that occasion was that the Burmese refused to acknowledge a debt of one thousand pounds, which led Richard Cobden to query 'ought we not to advertise in *The Times* for a Governor-General who can collect a debt of a thousand pounds without annexing a territory which will be ruinous to our finances?' (33).

With hindsight we know that most of the colonial conquests

made during the nineteenth century were neither economically necessary (34) nor even profitable for the colonial nation as a whole. But this is not so important, for a number of reasons. The decisions were determined by the then prevailing anxiety about saturated markets and protectionist competition. And even if the colonies were not profitable for the colonial power as such, they often provided lucrative returns for the ruling upper class. One should also bear in mind that it was the economic gains from earlier colonies that determined the assessment of future possibilities. Several of the colonial enterprises yielded fabulous dividends (35). Many of the great British private fortunes of today trace their origins to the heyday of the East India Company. During 150 years the Dutch East India Company paid dividends which never fell below 11.25 per cent (36). The above mentioned triangular trade between Europe, Africa and America was extremely profitable.

The effects of colonial policy in different regions varied. They did, however, have a few common features. All colonial powers attempted to make the activities in the colonies self-financing. Administration and other overheads were to be paid for by taxes and tariffs. The profits could be repatriated by the private enterprises. That was quite clearly the objective of British policy. Only the Netherlands pursued what one might call an outright policy of state exploitation (37). All colonial powers tried to adapt production in the colonies to the needs of the metropolis. The colonies were to produce raw materials for the industries of Europe and to remain markets for manufactured products. The cultivation of export crops was stimulated at the expense of self-sufficiency in foodstuffs. Industrial development was obstructed or banned.

In certain colonies an extensive administrative system was built up. India is perhaps the best example. In large parts of Africa, on the other hand, only the coastal regions were integrated in the economic systems of the colonial power prior to the First World War. In West Africa, for example, internal trade was chiefly in the hands of Africans during the nineteenth century. In the Caribbean and part of Southern and Eastern Africa, European settlers established extensive plantations. Through colonial taxes the required labour force was coerced into a precarious cash economy (38).

In many descriptions of colonialism, moral indignation has also coloured the economic picture. But the differences between various colonial regions is too great to permit any general conclusions. The British conquest of India led to substantially lower taxation for Hindu farmers who had been oppressed by a numerous Muslim ruling class for 700 years (39). In other areas new tariffs, taxes and charges were introduced in order to finance colonial administration and investment activities. The degree of integration into the capitalist world economy also varied greatly. In some colonies – and for that matter also in formally independent states in Latin America – attractive raw materials gave rise to enclave economies which were only loosely anchored in the self-sufficient domestic economy which predominated in those societies. In other areas peasants added to their cash incomes by producing for export. The most far-reaching interlocking with the world economy took place in those colonies where white colonists and corporations established plantations for the production of tropical commodities.

The economic perspective is too narrow, however. Colonialism represented above all an alien value system which had profound economic, social and cultural consequences in the societies affected by it. In parts of Asia, Africa and Latin America prior to modern colonialism the people lived in economically self-sufficient societies which had stabilised the population at the level determined by the productiveness of the soil and by the availability of game. This balance was often at a lower level than what was possible with known cultivation techniques. It appears as if several of these societies strove to maximise labour productivity. This involved limiting the population to the number that could be supported with a fairly modest effort. The methods of achieving this limitation varied. Sexual taboos – e.g. the prohibition of sexual intercourse during a nursing period of 3–5 years – were common, as were various abortion methods. Different ways of legitimising abortions also appear to have existed. The condition for the functioning of the system was that the land was collectively owned and that the food was distributed according to need.

This social pattern was undermined by colonial exploiters

and Christian missionaries. Abortion was combated. The growth in population and taxes necessitated heavier exploitation of the land, which required an increase in the labour input. The colonial powers introduced the private ownership of land. This removed the basis for the collective economy existing in several regions of Asia, Africa and Latin America. Differences of income rapidly increased. A privileged class emerged which adopted the culture and the scale of values of the colonial power.

Once the ecological balance had been disturbed there was no way back. The clearing of new land, improved techniques and more intensive agriculture were the only possibilities for satisfying an increasing demand. Development became a straitjacket (40).

Colonialism basically meant that the people in the Third World were deprived of the possibility of making their own choice of national development. They were allotted a given place in a European world order against which they were not able to revolt until the 1960s.

EMIGRATION AND THE EXPORT OF CAPITAL

Two distinctive characteristics of the internationalisation of the world economy during the nineteenth century were a massive export of private long-term capital and an emigration from Europe, which exceeded 10 per cent of the population of that continent. During the period 1815–1913 about 45 million Europeans, out of a population which simultaneously grew from 200 to 450 millions, moved to North America, Latin America, Australia, South Africa and New Zealand. The total gross outflow of capital during the same period amounted to $40–45 billions.

At the beginning of the nineteenth century foreign investments were small. Around the middle of the century over 2 billion dollars had been invested abroad. By 1870 this figure had trebled. But the great outflow wave of investment took place during the period 1870–1913. Then capital to a value of $37 billion was exported, chiefly from Great Britain (43 per cent), France (20 per cent) and Germany (13 per cent). The

most striking feature of this development was not so much the export of capital, which was imposing enough in itself, but its size in relation to total production and investments in the exporting and importing countries.

During the whole of the fifty-year period 1865–1914 the annual gross export of capital from Great Britain represented an average of 4.3 per cent of the country's total output; during the years 1905–13 the ratio reached 7 per cent and during the very last years of the period as much as 9 per cent (41). This meant that during the peak years Great Britain's export of capital was equivalent to over half of its available gross savings. For the period 1860–1913 as a whole, the export of capital constituted 25–40 per cent of the total accumulation of capital. For France, which during the period 1880–1914 trebled its foreign investments from $3 billion to $9 billion the relative figures were probably comparable with those of Great Britain. Germany staked less on foreign investments. Despite this its foreign investments increased from just over $1.2 billion in 1880 to nearly $6 billion in 1914 (42).

Total foreign investments increased in fixed prices during 1874–1913 from $4.9 billion to $35.3 billion. This rate of growth of 64 per cent per decade clearly exceeded the growth in world trade during the same period (43). The annual outflow of capital corresponded to about one tenth of the volume of world trade (44).

Part of the explanation for this outflow of capital is political. Governments attempted to stimulate investments in newly acquired colonies or to give financial support to their allies in the face of the war that threatened in Europe. The chief explanation, however, must have been that the investments yielded a good return. The return flows of interests, instalments and dividends soon amounted to considerable sums. During the later part of the nineteenth century both Great Britain and France became net receivers of capital, which allowed them to maintain a considerable deficit in their balance of trade. India, i.e. the present India, Pakistan and Bangladesh, was soon turned into a net exporter of capital. Angus Maddison has calculated that the annual net export of capital from India to Great Britain amounted to a sum corresponding to 1.5 per cent of the national income of the subcontinent in the early 1920s. A part of this sum consisted of so-called 'home charges', i.e. 'compensation' to the colonial power for its administration (45). S. B. Saul has characterised the role of India before the first world war as 'the key to Britain's whole payments pattern . . . financing, as she probably did, more than two-fifths of Britain's total deficits' (46).

The export surplus required to achieve this feat was largely obtained by the profitable export of opium from India to China (47). As late as 1870 half of China's imports consisted of opium. For the Netherlands the Indonesian possessions were extremely important (48). Only a minor part of the exports and investments of the colonial powers were, however, absorbed by their own colonies. Great Britain's investments in India, Ceylon and in African colonies, excluding South Africa, amounted to about 10 per cent of total foreign investments. Hardly any German capital went to the colonial possessions, and the French investments in the colonies formed less than a tenth of the total value of the country's foreign investments in 1914. Though the United States' investments before 1914 were concentrated in its own hemisphere, only insignificant investments were made in its colonies (49).

The bulk of the capital investments was placed in Europe and North America. These regions counted for over half of the foreign gross investments outstanding in 1913. About one-fifth were in Latin America and 5 per cent in Australia and New Zealand.

Capital exported to Australia, New Zealand, South Africa and Canada formed about half of the total investments in those countries during the 1880s and 1890s (50). The United States financed about 10 per cent of its accumulation of capital through loans from abroad in the period immediately prior to 1913. In Japan the import of capital during the period 1897–1906 represented almost one third of investments. In the Scandinavian countries, too, foreign loans played a decisive role in financing railway construction and other infrastructural investments. In Russia half of the total share capital and an equivalent proportion of the national debt were in foreign hands at the beginning of the twentieth century.

In some respects the world economy was an integrated and functioning whole to a greater extent during the decades before 1914 than in any earlier and perhaps (?) later epoch of equivalent length. The effects of industrialisation in the early industrial metropolises spread like rings on the water to the countries on the periphery.

In the earliest industrialised countries a capital surplus was generated which was lent out for investments in countries which started later. In North America, South Africa, Australia, New Zealand and large parts of Latin America the capital inflow was accompanied by a large-scale immigration of Europeans.

Exports calculated as a proportion of the gross national product reached a level at the beginning of the twentieth century which most industrial countries were not to reach again until late in the 1960s (51). It took an oil crisis, with its sudden redistribution of the world's liquid financial resources, to match the level of private capital flows during the decades before the Great War. Emigration took on the nature of mass population movements.

The stability of the system was guaranteed by Great Britain, which by a consistent free trade policy and growing imports enabled the countries which had borrowed capital to finance its repayments through export surpluses.

The export of capital consisted largely of long-term loans, often to governments for investments in railways, power supply and public social services. Only to a minor extent did the capital movements constitute direct investments, with subsequent control of the production facilities. Direct investments made before 1913 were with few exceptions in mines and plantations.

WHY DID NOT ALL COUNTRIES DEVELOP?

A central question — which can only be touched upon here — is why only a minority of the 'developing countries' of the nineteenth century — the Scandinavian countries, the United States, Australia, New Zealand, Japan and a few others — were able to benefit permanently from their collaboration with the major industrial countries and to establish a selfsustained expansion. One important reason is that these countries often started from a higher income level than other countries, had greater resources of cultivable land, a superior education system, a functioning state apparatus and a superior standard of health.

A more obvious reason is the colonial system. The Scandinavian countries, Canada, Japan, Australia and New Zealand were established national states with a functioning administration themselves. The colonial regions were subordinated to the economic systems of the metropolitan countries, which often involved outright prohibitions against the establishment of competing exports of manufactured products. Several of these regions also arose through arbitrary colonial partitioning, comprising peoples of different cultures, languages and religions, and thus lacking natural cohesive bonds.

These explanations do not cover all the cases, however. The Latin American countries were independent from the beginning of the nineteenth century, many of them experienced a rapid rise in export demand, and some of them had a GNP per capita which was higher than Sweden's and far higher than Japan's. Simon Kuznets points to one possible explanation when he says that the redistributive effects were delayed:

'by a political and institutional framework which . . . permitted the small elites to profit from the economic advantages of their position without embodying strong incentives and pressures for change that would spread the benefits and lay the foundations for greater modernization of the economic and social structure' (52).

But the problem was not only small local elites which lacked any concern for a broad national development. The export enclaves which were created in Latin America, concentrated in coastal cities or rich mineral zones, were often under foreign control. One example was the guano industry (53) in Peru which was financed by European capital, used Chinese manpower, shipped out the produce in English vessels and was entirely dependent on foreign markets (54).

The flow of capital to colonies and countries in Latin America was to a considerable extent linked with investments in raw material extraction. This meant that the redistributive effects were exceedingly small or even negative. The capital equipment was imported. Few employment opportunities were created. As late as 1960 when 40 per cent of exports from developing countries consisted of mineral products, this sector provided only 0.6 per cent of employment – and half of this was supplied by the extraction of stone, gravel and sand (55). Investments in transport not only facilitated the export of minerals and internal transport but they also opened up the market for the importation of cheap mass-produced goods from the industrial countries. And the profits were repatriated to the mother country. It is perhaps not so surprising that some researchers have found a clear negative connection between rapid growth of extractive industries and the development of a manufacturing industry (56).

Another reason why countries in Latin America, Asia and Africa did not reach the stage of self-sustaining growth was that the capital that they could borrow was very expensive. The nominal interest might in itself appear to be modest, but as the bonds were often sold at far below par the real interest was high. In several cases these countries were forced to raise loans in order to pay off previous debts. Added to this were the substantial profits from commission fees appropriated by European bankers. Several of today's developing countries went through debt-repayment even before the Great War.

It was the industrialisation process during the nineteenth century which created the basis for the dramatic gaps that exist today between rich and poor countries. Before industrialisation got under way the industrialised countries of today had a gross national product per inhabitant which was 2–3 times larger than the average for countries in Asia and Africa. Measured by the same traditional yardstick (57) it is today about 15 times larger. More thorough calculations, in which the cost of living is taken into account, show smaller discrepancies, but the fact remains – the process of modernisation which began in Europe at the end of the eighteenth century and gave the countries which were industrialised at an early stage the political and economic dominion over the rest of the world is the principal cause of the injustices which lie behind the demands by the poor countries for a new international economic order.

ECONOMIC DEVELOPMENT BETWEEN THE WARS

The rapid growth of the world industrial output continued during the first part of the interwar period. This development was particularly marked in the United States and Japan, while Great Britain's industrial output stagnated completely. The rapid expansion in the USA was supported by an explosive development of the automobile industry, which almost trebled the number of vehicles manufactured during the 1920s. Great Britain had developed rapidly during the war, when a series of new industries were established and new products were developed. An immediate return to a phlegmatic *laissez faire* policy, however, prevented the potential of the war effort from being utilized. The problems of the export industry were aggravated by the fact that the pound was overvalued.

The war led to an increased need to import materials from the colonies. At the same time their difficulties in obtaining industrial products from Europe forced them to industrialise. The Indian steel industry was given a strong boost. The exploitation of tungsten in Burma, rubber in Malaya and copper in the Congo and Rhodesia accelerated during the war.

World trade increased more slowly during the twenties than before the war. This was due *inter alia* to high tariffs and the network of debts and claims to which the Great War had given rise. France and Great Britain demanded enormous war reparations from Germany, which the latter was quite incapable of paying. Great Britain had claims against its allies, which they counted on being able to pay out of the reparations received from Germany. And that in its turn was the precondition for Great Britain being able to pay its debts to the United States. This situation was provisionally regulated through the so-called Dawes Plan of 1924. Such trade as nevertheless did get going was to a large extent financed with American and British credits (58).

The depression of the thirties led to a drastic slowing down

Table 2   Index for total world industrial production 1870-1938.

	1870	1913	1929	1938
Total world industrial production (index 1913 = 100)	20	100	153	183
United States	13	100	181	143
Germany	16	100	117	117
Great Britain	44	100	100	108
Japan	–	100	324	552
India	–	100	157	240
Sweden	8	100	151	232

Source: Bünte & Jorberg, p. 33

Table 3   Growth of world trade 1913-37.

	1913	1928	1937
Volume of world trade (index 1913 = 100)	100	113	114

Source: Kuznets (1966), p. 308.

of industrial activity. According to calculations made by the League of Nations, world industrial output fell by one third during 1929-32 (59). Thirty million people were thrown out of work in the rich countries. The cause of the crisis was thought to be overproduction and the remedy was taken for granted. Enormous supplies of foodstuffs were destroyed in order to raise the price of the food that starving workers could not afford to buy. The leading economists of the period devoted very little attention to analysing the causes of unemployment, as it could not exist according to their theories (that is actually true) (60).

The effects were most immediate in the United States, where the total output of industry was almost halved. US foreign lending ceased completely and with that the international economy collapsed. The depression also gave rise to a wave of protectionism. World trade decreased by 65 per cent between the first quarter of 1929 and the first quarter of 1933 (61). During the years immediately before the Second World War the volume of world trade had reached a level which was only about 10 per cent higher than in 1913.

In 1929 the United States accounted for 42 per cent of world

Table 4   Geographical   distribution   of   world   industrial production 1870-1938.

	1870 %	1913 %	1926-29 %	1936-38 %
United States	23.3	35.8	42.2	32.2
Germany	13.2	15.7	11.6	10.7
Great Britain	31.8	14.0	9.4	9.2
France	10.3	6.4	6.6	4.5
Russia/Soviet Union (62)	3.7	5.5	4.3	18.5
Sweden	0.4	1.0	1.0	1.3
Japan	–	1.2	2.5	3.5
India	–	1.1	1.2	1.4
Other countries	–	18.3	21.2	18.7

Source: Hilgerdt, p. 13

industrial output. This share fell to about one third by 1938. The other major industrial countries by and large retained their shares. A rise in production, and thereby in relative position, occurred primarily in the Soviet Union and Japan.

The depression struck the developing countries initially through the radical reduction in demand for primary commodities. This caused difficulties for the heavily indebted countries of Latin America. Several of them attempted to cope with the problems by devaluing their currencies and substituting domestic industrial production for previously imported goods. These measures, which continued during the Second World War, created the basis for the large share of the industrial output of the Third World which is held by Latin American countries today.

The depression did not cause any radical change in the international trading pattern if one looks at aggregate total figures. The shares of Western Europe and North America fell a little during the period 1928–37. The increased production of the USSR was utilised for domestic purposes. The participation of the USSR in international trade diminished. It is worth noting that the two poorest continents increased their share of world exports during the inter-war period. Even if the Asian increase is largely explained by advances in Japanese exports, the statistics accommodate increased exports also from other countries in the region.

Most of the developing countries in Latin America and Asia were forced during the whole of the inter-war period to create a surplus in their balance of trade in order to pay interest, debt instalments and the costs of administration by colonial powers. The countries in Western Asia and Africa had considerable deficits.

The stable distribution of world trade between primary commodities and manufactured products was maintained during the inter-war period. In 1938 raw materials constituted 63–64 per cent of total trade, i.e. about the same proportion as during the period 1876–1913. In the years before the depression the share of raw materials was about 61-62 per cent.

Large-scale emigration from Europe continued during the first half of the inter-war period. Nearly 50 per cent of the emigrants found their way to the United States and Canada. Other major destinations for emigrants were Argentina, Brazil and Australia.

One important difference compared with the period before the Great War concerned international capital movements. Before 1925 loans were granted mainly under government auspices, often through the League of Nations. After that private capital flows picked up again, only to cease almost completely as a result of the depression.

Great Britain could not maintain its export of capital on the pre-war level. Instead the United States emerged as the dominant exporter of capital. American investments abroad increased during 1920–30 from 7 to 17 billion dollars. Roughly half consisted of direct investments, about 50 per cent of which went to developing countries.

The portfolio investments were concentrated in Western Europe and Canada. Great Britain and France were still net exporters of capital, while several other European countries, above all Germany, raised large loans abroad.

A WORLD ORDER COMES INTO BEING

The Second World War brought about a radical shift in the balance of power between the world's leading industrial states, both in military and economic respects. The United States emerged from its isolationism of the inter-war period as the

Table 5   Balance of trade for non-communist developing countries 1913–38 (millions of U.S. dollars)

	1913	1928	1938
Developing countries in Latin America			
Exports	1,600	3,100	1,710
Imports	1,450	2,450	1,540
Surplus or deficit	+ 150	+ 650	+ 170
Surplus or deficit as percentage of imports	+ 10.3%	+ 26.5%	+ 11.0%
Developing countries in the Middle East			
Exports	330	630	550
Imports	410	630	720
Surplus of deficit	− 80	−	−170
Surplus of deficit as percentage of imports	− 19.5%	−	− 23.6%
Other developing countries in Asia			
Exports	1,550	3,140	2,650
Imports	1,250	2,500	2,370
Surplus or deficit	+ 300	+ 640	+ 280
Surplus or deficit as percentage of imports	+ 29.0%	+ 25.6%	+ 11.8%
Developing countries in Africa			
Exports	250	590	660
Imports	330	690	670
Surplus or deficit	− 80	−100	− 10
Surplus or deficit as percentage of imports	− 24.2%	−14.5%	− 1.5%

Source: Bairoch, p. 97

world's dominant great power with definite plans to make the world 'safe for capitalism'.

The US had not only financed its whole war effort through increased production. The planned economy necessitated by the war mobilisation had also solved the problems of the thirties and provided scope for increased civilian production. The federal budget rose from $9 billion in 1939 to $100 billion in 1945, about 17 million jobs were created and the total output was doubled (63). American enterprises could without difficulty take over markets which had previously been dominated by European and Japanese exporters. They captured for instance the profitable Latin American market for medical goods, in which German enterprises had previously been in a strong position (64). Generous federal orders and subsidies for R & D further increased the lead of the American enterprises in the struggle for export markets in the postwar period.

At the end of the war the United States alone accounted for about one-third of the world's total output. Several years after the war a third of the world's exports still came from the United States, which at the same time took only about one-tenth of world imports (65). The export surplus corresponded to 4 per cent of its GNP. The rest of the world lost 25 per cent of its gold and currency reserves during the years 1946–47 alone (66). The flow of gold across the Atlantic had gathered momentum when Hitler came to power and by 1948 the Americans controlled three-quarters of the world's monetary gold as compared with one third in 1933 (67).

Great Britain, which in the years before the war had still been the world's leading trading nation and financial centre, was forced to draw on all available resources for its war effort. Exports were cut down to a third of the pre-war level (68), imports were financed by lend-lease aid from the United States and Canada, and a considerable part of its overseas assets were sold. With worn-down and partly destroyed production facilities, a third of its merchant marine lost (69), insignificant currency reserves, its capital earnings from abroad halved (70), and large debts to the colonies for deliveries during the war, Great Britain was in urgent need of large credits for its economic development.

France, like Great Britain, had ceased to be an international creditor. The need to borrow money in order to reconstruct its industry was acute. The previous major exporters, Germany and Japan, were ruined, put in political quarantine and dependent on imports even for the necessities of life. In 1948 industrial output in Japan was still at one-third and in Germany at half of the pre-war level.

Among the Allies the Soviet Union was hardest hit by the war. Between 15 and 20 million Russians lost their lives — about two-thirds of the total losses in human lives during the war. The industrial installations and infrastructure were destroyed over large parts of the country.

International problems were aggravated by the fact that the countries and colonies in Asia could not, as had happened after the Great War, replace a certain part of the loss of output in

Europe. These countries had also been hit by the war, and the rapid increase of population was beginning to eliminate their food surplus which had previously been exported.

Many smaller countries whose industry and agriculture remained intact — e.g. Sweden, Canada and several Latin American states — took advantage of the sellers' market which arose. But only the United States had the productive capacity to match the enormous requirements.

The domination of the United States was thus unchallenged — and in addition the Americans had the advantage of knowing how they wanted to shape a new world order. For all the other belligerents the war had been literally a life and death struggle. All decisions were subordinated to military needs, the war effort had the highest priority in relation to all resources. But the United States was never threatened militarily and the planning for the world economy of the postwar period began even before Pearl Harbor (71).

The fundamental idea which determined a large part of the American government's planning was that the country needed overseas export markets for a surplus of production which was estimated to be at least $10 billions (72). The then Assistant Secretary of State, Dean Acheson, expressed a common point of view when he told a committee of the House of Representatives in 1944 that 'no group which has studied this problem, and there have been many, as you know, has ever believed that our domestic markets could absorb our entire production under our present system' (73).

Apparently nobody considered that the Keynesian policy which had been applied during the war could work also in peacetime. But that was of little importance, as Congress was obsessed with the idea of a balanced federal budget. When the armaments contracts ceased, the industry would be left without orders and agriculture would again produce the surplus which had contributed to the depression in the thirties. To achieve a sufficiently large export surplus became the key to the whole economic postwar programme — which was supposed to save the world from communism and the United States from unemployment.

One goal was thus taken for granted. World trade had to be liberalised, all obstacles to imports removed and competition on equal terms allowed. Among other things the United States was concerned about the fact that several developing countries had started to build up their industry under the protection of high tariffs and the wartime blockade. According to a report published in 1943 this could lead to 'the permanent loss of some of this country's export outlets' (74).

Another important source of irritation was the colonial trade preferences, above all those of the British Commonwealth, which discriminated against external exporters. The British had made it plain that they might have to reinforce these arrangements after the war in order to cope with their balance of payments. In the Atlantic Charter of 1941 the two countries had agreed on a compromise, according to which they would work for a liberalisation of the world economy 'with due respect for their existing obligations' (75). This did not satisfy public opinion in the United States, however, and the lend-lease treaty that was signed in February 1942 forced the British to accept the famous clause VII which prescribed, *inter alia*, that the two countries should jointly work towards 'the elimination of all forms of discriminatory treatment in international commerce' (75). This was a compromise that was interpreted differently in Washington and London. The dissatisfied Congress was, however, soothed with an assurance that this was directed against imperial preferences as well as against future regional trading blocs.

There were powerful forces in the United States that wished to press the British even harder. One popular idea was to acquire proportions of the British oil fields in the Middle East in exchange for lend-lease deliveries. This would satisfy another important goal — namely to give all enterprises access to the world's sources of raw materials on equal terms. The government in Washington was aware, however, that it needed the support of the British to win the other European countries for the American economic postwar programme.

Another central element in this programme was a stable currency system. Fixed exchange rates and a prescribed procedure to change them would prevent 'unnecessary' devaluations. The principal goal was to make the national currencies freely convertible for current payments, which is a condition for free trade. It soon became evident that these goals could not be achieved immediately. When the Americans forced Great Britain to make the pound convertible a few years after the war, this had catastrophic repercussions. The experiment lasted for five weeks and cost the British $700 million (76). A reconstruction of the postwar economy on American conditions required American credits; of that the government in Washington, though not Congress, was already convinced by the end of the war.

Nor was there any doubt that the United States intended to assume control over the reconstruction of the world economy. A return to the isolationism of the thirties was never a realistic alternative. 'We should assume this leadership, and the responsibility that goes with it, primarily for reasons of pure national self-interest', Secretary of State Cordell Hull observed (77).

This firm resolve was strengthened by the Cold War. Initially the Americans had formulated their plans with a view to co-operation, which also embraced the Soviet Union. Several of the architects of the postwar era within the administration regarded this as both desirable and necessary. Fairly soon, however, it became apparent that this plan was impossible. For the United States, cooperation meant trade on equal terms and free movements of capital. Stalin saw all foreign relations from the narrow perspective of security policy and this did not include free trade in Eastern Europe.

Two competing world orders were emerging, and very soon the struggle against communism became the overrriding aim of the economic postwar strategy of the United States.

The institutional framework

After the war a series of negotiations began in order to create an International Trade Organization (ITO) (78). A government agreement on ITO was concluded at a conference in Havana in the winter of 1947–48.

Pending the coming into force of the ITO agreement* 23

---

* The treaty of Havana was signed by the negotiating delegates of the participating governments. The condition for the coming into force of the treaty was that the parliaments of a sufficient number of countries should accept (ratify) it.

countries met in Geneva in 1947 for trade negotiations. These were conducted on a bilateral basis but the liberalising measures agreed upon were extended to cover all participating countries. The results were incorporated in the General Agreement on Tariffs and Trade (GATT).

ITO died at birth. In 1950 the Truman administration abandoned its attempts to persuade a recalcitrant Congress. GATT, the substitute, became the predominant international trade organisation.

Formally GATT remains a multilateral agreement covering rules for trade between the member countries. In fact, however, it is an established organisation with its own administration and a number of tasks in the sphere of trade. Its main task has always been to contribute to freer world trade by reducing tariffs and other obstacles to trade.

The main principle of GATT is the so-called most favoured nation clause. This implies that every trading advantage, such as lowering of tariffs on certain products, granted by one country to another should also apply to all other member countries. One consequence of this is that all kinds of preferential arrangements are banned as a matter of principle.

Another important GATT principle is that domestic industry may only be protected by tariffs. This clause is aimed at preventing such measures as quantitative restrictions and subsidies. The agreement also prescribes that participating countries should consult with each other on various questions concerning obstacles to trade. In principle GATT applies to all trade; but at an early stage the United States forced an exception to be made for agricultural products. In practice, therefore, GATT has become an agreement on trade in industrial products (79).

The membership of GATT increased rapidly — most of the developing countries that were independent in the 1960s joined — and trade negotiations were arranged at regular intervals. In this way a liberalisation of world trade was gradually achieved. The Kennedy Round in the mid 1960s led to a decision to reduce tariffs on industrial goods by more than 30 per cent over a five-year period (80). This led to a situation where tariffs no longer appeared to be the decisive trading obstacles for the major part of international trade in manufactured products.

The attempt by the United States to bring about a liberalisation of trade presupposed large-scale international credits
and an orderly monetary system. As early as December 1941
Harry Dexter White, special adviser to the United States Secretary of the Treasury, Morgenthau, presented a plan for
'Inter Allied Monetary and Bank Action'. At about the same
time John Maynard Keynes in Great Britain put forward his
ideas about a 'clearing union' (a kind of international central
bank) with resources amounting to $26 billions and responsi-
bility for an international monetary system called 'bancor'.
Both proposals aimed at a radical new arrangement of the
world's currency system and foresaw a large-scale need of
credits for reconstruction in Europe.

White's plan was immediately subjected to extensive revision
within the administration, however. And the proposal which
the American government submitted to other countries in
November 1943 was considerably more modest and — as it was
to turn out later — quite inadequate to meet the problems of
the postwar period.

The supporters of the New Deal were on the retreat within
the administration. The big banks were decidedly sceptical
about large-scale government credits to overseas countries.
And in Congress the influential senator Robert Taft feared
that the plans under discussion were really some new schemes
for 'deficit financing' (81).

Credits could only come from the United States. Any proposal must therefore be such that the American government
could persuade Congress to accept it. Generally speaking, it
was only the British government that was consulted when the
final plans were worked out. In the spring of 1944 an agreement
on the monetary questions was reached which largely followed
American wishes. The question as to whether a bank should
be established at the same time remained uncertain up to the
last moment. In the invitation to the final conference at Bretton
Woods, New Hampshire, which Morgenthau issued to 44
countries, its purpose was defined as that 'of formulating
definite proposals for an International Monetary Fund and
possibly a Bank for Reconstruction and Development' (82).

This conference, which took place in the summer of 1944, amounted by and large to an endorsement by the participating countries of the American–British plans for the international monetary system of the postwar period. Even the Soviet Union, which strove to gain as much influence as possible over the fund, was among the signatory powers. It was clear at an early stage, however, that Moscow would not ratify it.

The most important outcome of the Bretton Woods conference was the regulations for the world system of payments and currencies which were written into the charter of the International Monetary Fund (IMF). The new order consisted of the following elements:

— fixed exchange rates (the currency of each country was given a par value, which was indicated in gold or in dollars, at the gold value of the dollar in 1944; the currency rate was allowed to vary from the par value by at most 1 per cent)
— a procedure was adopted for the alterations of exchange rates that might become necessary
— all currencies were to be freely convertible
— loans could only be granted to finance temporary deficits
— if a currency became scarce, the fund could allow member countries to limit imports from the country of issue of that currency (a rule that has never been applied) (83)
— each country was given a so-called quota in the fund. This was determined by the country's GNP, foreign trade and currency reserves. The quota is significant in several respects. It determines voting rights and borrowing facilities, It also determines how much each country is to pay into the fund. Twenty five per cent of the quota was originally to be paid in gold and the remainder in the local currency.

The Bretton Woods conference also managed to agree on establishing a bank for reconstruction and development, i.e. the World Bank (International Bank for Reconstruction and Development, IBRD). This was partly due to the fact that the United States realised that the bank was needed as a bait to induce certain countries, in particular the Latin American ones, to join the fund. It was decided that membership of the bank should be open only to countries participating in the fund. The immediate task of the bank was to supply credits for reconstruction in Europe. Right from the start, however, it was made clear, in the words of Keynes, that it had 'a second primary duty laid upon it, namely to develop the resources and productive capacity of the world, with special reference to the less developed countries' (84).

The resources of the Bretton Woods institutions were, however, far too small to cope with the postwar problems. The aggregate quotas of the fund were fixed at Bretton Woods at slightly over $8 billion, but this included the Soviet Union, and the final result was less than $7 billions. Only some of the currencies were attractive to borrowers and could be obtained only on special conditions. Up to the mid-1950s total drawings from the fund* were to remain below $2 billions.

The aggregate 'authorised' capital of the World Bank amounted at the start to an impressive $10 billions. This was distributed between the member countries in roughly the same proportion as the quotas in the fund. But 80 per cent consisted of guaranteed capital and could only be utilised to cover losses. Two per cent should be paid in gold or dollars and the remainder in a national currency, which could only be used for lending if the donor country gave its consent. When the bank began to operate, therefore, it had at its disposal only the paid-up share of the United States' contribution, i.e. less than $600 millions (85). The main problem of the bank was thus, as the *Economist* pointed out, 'to find not borrowers, but lenders prepared to accept reasonable terms' (86).

The bank simply had to be accepted in Wall Street — and this fact of life was to govern its development for a long time to come. The American banks had to be convinced that the IBRD was not a competitor but that, on the contrary, it promoted private loans and investments. When the first loan to Chile came up for consideration, the bank made it clear that a settlement of that country's prewar debts was an absolute condition. And the

---

* Strictly speaking the fund does not grant loans. It sells currencies. This is done by one country depositing its own currency and receiving the equivalent in the currency of another country. A country's right to make these drawings is determined by the size of its quota and what proportion of it has already been taken up.

head of the bank declared in April 1948 that the bank's main task was to 'blaze the trail for private international investment' (87).

The era which began during the first years after the war has sometimes been called the Bretton Woods epoch. This is hardly warranted. It was the United States which controlled the world's financial and monetary system. The World Bank's credits were quite insignificant compared to the loans granted by the United States — bilaterally and through the UN relief organisation UNRRA (United Nations Relief and Rehabilitation Administration) — to Europe, Japan and the developing countries. Great Britain received a loan of $3.75 billions immediately after the war. UNRRA provided assistance to the amount of $3 billions, two thirds of which were paid by the United States. Through Marshall Aid, which was introduced in the summer of 1948, the United States supplied grants and loans totalling $12.5 billions to Europe and Japan over four years.

The International Monetary Fund began to operate in 1947 with a dream about the monetary system entirely divorced from reality. Five years later only six countries were able to apply the rules for trade and international payments which were laid down in article VIII of the fund agreement. Limited drawings were made during the first year of operation before Marshall Aid took over. Only at the end of the 1950s, when all industrial countries of any significance made their currencies convertible, did the system begin to work in accordance with the original intentions (88). By that time one of the fundamental weaknesses of the fund was also apparent — it lacked rules on how and to what extent international liquidity should be increased. This important central banking task was primarily handled by the United States. Through a deficit in the balance of payments of that country the rest of the world was supplied with an average of $600 millions a year during the period 1949–59 (89). This meant quite simply that the United States could unilaterally decide to raise cheap loans from the rest of the world by printing dollar bills. All the dollars in circulation represented a claim on the American economy. The holder could use them to buy commodities, to convert them into gold or to invest them in so-called treasury bills. It is not surprising that the Americans wished to maintain this favourable position and, when reforms of the currency system began to be discussed, Secretary of the Treasury Douglas Dillon declared in 1961 that the United States intended to preserve its role 'as the banker of the world' (90).

Economic recovery in Europe and Japan

The immediate problems in Europe and Japan concerned the bare necessities of life: food, clothing and housing. UNRRA was expressly prohibited by the American Congress from using its resources for reconstruction (91).

Economic activity in Europe was feeble. The countries were forced to ration their limited dollar holdings drastically. The United States' chances of achieving its export targets and avoiding unemployment required large-scale interventions to increase the purchasing power of the rest of the world. At the same time it was clear — in the primitive outlook that dominated Congress and the government — that Europe faced an immediate communist threat. The result was a marriage of convenience between aid and security policy — Marshall Aid. The reconstruction in Europe had to be undertaken in order to restore the balance of the world economy (92).

In April 1948 the American Congress adopted the Economic Cooperation Act, which came into force at once (93). Under this act American aid to the rest of the world could increase significantly, while at the same time the element of outright grants became predominant. Another major aid donor was Canada which, for instance, gave a loan of $2 billions to Great Britain (94). Marshall Aid alone corresponded to 5 per cent of the GNP of the receiving countries and 2 per cent of that of the United States — a circumstance that the world's really poor countries later had occasion to point out.

Assistance on this scale must reasonably have contributed to the rapid recovery of industry and agriculture that got under way at the end of the 1940s. It is difficult, however, to distinguish between the effects of aid and domestic measures. In the East European countries, which declined Marshall Aid for political reasons, the industrial recovery took place, if anything, more quickly than in Western Europe. An important reason for the recovery of the West European countries was presumably the devaluations which were carried out in September 1949. Great Britain, Denmark, Finland, the Netherlands, Norway and Sweden then depreciated their currencies by 30 per cent against the dollar. France and West Germany chose to devalue by 22 per cent and 20 per cent respectively. Most of the countries in the so-called sterling bloc followed Great Britain (95). This made imports from the United States more expensive and strengthened the competitive edge *vis-a-vis* American enterprises. A sharp rise in productivity in the economies of the West European countries also contributed to the gradual restoration of balance in the world economy (96).

Table 6   Industrial production 1938–60 (index 1953 = 100).

Year	Whole world	United States	Soviet Union	Great Britain	France	Japan	Federal Republic of Germany	Sweden	India
1938	52	34	30	76	75	96	(77)	62	76
1948	73	75	47	84	76	36	40	89	87
1953	100	100	100	100	100	100	100	100	100
1957	121	110	155	114	138	167	146	117	130
1960	139	119	206	126	161	261	179	130	161

Source: Bunte & Jorberg, p. 40.

The world order begins to function

The percentage increase in GDP which occurred during the years of reconstruction was exceptional in several respects. But even when economic conditions were stabilised the West European countries were able to sustain a higher economic growth rate than during any preceding period. In the 1950s the GDP per inhabitant in Western Europe increased by 3.5 per cent a year on average. This was twice as much as the American economy could achieve. In Japan the growth was even more rapid than in Western Europe.

As we mentioned earlier, the Soviet Union had increased its output very rapidly during the whole inter-war period. Its growth rate probably did not accelerate during the postwar period. But several East European countries did in the early postwar period increase their output at a rate close to 10 per cent a year.

Table 7   Annual rate of growth of GDP per capita in ten
European countries and United States 1870–1960.

Country	1870–1913 %	1913–50 %	1950–60 %
Belgium	1.7	0.7	2.3
Denmark	2.1	1.1	2.6
France	1.4	0.7	3.5
Federal Republic of Germany*	1.8	0.4	6.5
Italy	0.7	0.6	5.3
The Netherlands	0.8**	0.7	3.6
Norway	1.4	1.9	2.6
Sweden	2.3	1.6	2.6
Switzerland	1.3***	1.5	3.7
Great Britain	1.3	1.3	2.2
Average for ten European countries	1.5	1.0	3.5
United States	2.2	1.7	1.6

Source: Maddison (1964), p. 30.

*   For 1870–1913 and 1913–50 the figures refer to the former German Reich.
**   1900–1913.
*** 1890–1913.

In the 1960s the growth rate accelerated further in the majority of countries in the world. The GDP of the industrialised countries grew by about 5 per cent a year and by about 3.5–4 per cent per capita. The average annual increase of production in developing countries which in the 1950s was less than 5 per cent approached 6 per cent at the end of the sixties. Due to the rapid increase of population, however, the per capita growth achieved by the developing countries remained at 2.5–3 per cent a year. The East European countries increased their production in the 1960s by 6–7 per cent a year (97).

In terms of international trade, too, a rapid expansion began quite soon after the war and towards the end of the 1950s most Western European countries had recovered their 'historic' shares of the world trade. In 1960 Western Europe accounted for about 38 per cent of total exports compared with some 40 per cent in 1929. The United States' share at both of these dates was exactly the same, approximately 16 per cent. The developing countries' share of world exports diminished markedly during the 1950s, mainly due to rapidly falling prices of primary commodities.

Total world trade increased much more rapidly during the 1950s than total output. This tendency was reinforced during the 1960s. While the world's aggregate output of goods and services rose by 70 per cent in real terms the volume of world trade increased by almost 115 per cent. The internationalisation of the world economy again began to reach the proportions that it had before the First World War.

One factor controbuting to this development was the marked increase in foreign investments which took place in the 1960s.

Immediately after the Second World War production in foreign-owned enterprises formed a relatively smaller proportion of the world economy than, for example, at the end of the nineteenth century. Great Britain had been forced to liquidate foreign assets during the war. In 1946 the United States' foreign investments corresponded to only 3.4 per cent of its GDP — and immediately after the war its home market and exports were more attractive than risky ventures abroad. During the 1950s the private outflow of capital from the United States increased rather slowly. Thereafter a rapid expansion took place during the sixties, clearly directed towards the European Common Market. In 1970 foreign assets of American enterprises corresponded to 8 per cent of GDP, which was somewhat higher than in 1914 and 1929 (98). Along with the United States, Great Britain began to resume its role as an exporter of capital in the 1950s.

American and British enterprises still dominate the investments by the OECD countries in the developing countries. The outflow of new investment capital from these two countries has, however, increased more slowly than from several other industrial countries particularly since the mid-1960s. The value of the foreign investments of American enterprises decreased, when calculated as a proportion of the United States' GNP, during the period 1965–76. During this period it was above all Japanese and West German enterprises that expanded abroad. Enterprises in the Netherlands, Belgium and the Scandinavian countries also increased their foreign investments relatively quickly (99).

The total book value of foreign direct investments stood at about $165 billions in 1971 and the total production of foreign-owned enterprises was calculated at $330 billions. In 1967 rather less than a third of all private foreign investments were located in developing countries. The foreign-controlled production in these countries may thus be calculated at over $100 billions in 1971, which then corresponded to about one fifth of the GNP of developing countries' GNP. The corresponding share for industrialised countries was about 10 per cent.

At the end of the 1940s about 55 per cent of all private foreign investments in the developing countries had been made in agriculture or in the extractive industries. Since then the transnational enterprises have extended their interests to more and more sectors. Concerning the tendencies during the 1960s the UN report, Multinational Corporations in World Development, has the following to say:

'Generally speaking, the relative importance of the multinational corporation in developing countries is rising in the manufacturing and services sectors and declining in the primary industries, in particular those connected with agriculture (plantations). On balance, the overall importance of the multinational corporation is growing' (100).

Roughly speaking a quarter of the foreign investments in developing countries are now in the extractive sector, another quarter in service industries, and the remaining half in manufacturing industry.

There are widely differing opinions about the role and significance of the international corporations. Sanjaya Lall and Paul Streeten, who have made an extensive study of a large number of transnational enterprises, thus assert, in quoting the US Tariff Commission, that 'it is beyond dispute that the spread of multinational business ranks with the development of the steam engine, electric power and the automobile as one of the major events of modern economic history' (101).

In an appendix to the report of the Swedish Commission of Inquiry into Monopolies the economist Nils Lundgren adopts a decidedly more reserved position. Among other things he points out that 'the share of world output from plants owned by foreign business groups has not significantly increased during the sixties' (102). It is possible that the transnational enterprises are a kind of 'dinosaur doomed to decline in a new climate to which they are not adapted' (103).

   Economic development during the 1950s — and above all the fact that productivity increased much more rapidly in Europe and Japan than in the United States — made it possible for the overriding currency problem — the dollar shortage — to be resolved far more quickly than expected. It all happened so quickly in fact that it went unnoticed that the problem under discussion had already been resolved. The surplus in the American balance of trade was reduced from $10 billions in 1948 to $2.6 billions in 1952. And this latter sum was less than the outflow of dollars for investments and military and civilian aid (104). In the official statistical reporting of the United States' balance of payments, as it was then applied, a surplus was still indicated however (105). As late as in the mid-1950s serious discussions were devoted to an attempt to remedy the dollar shortage. Only during the last years of the decade did it begin to dawn that the reverse was the problem — the deficits in the United States' balance of payments increased and the gold reserves that guaranteed the dollar dwindled at an alarming rate.

   About the middle of the 1960s the large defence contracts for the Vietnam war began. This accelerated inflation. The faith in the dollar, which ultimately rested on the Americans' guarantee that it could be converted into gold at a fixed price, was thereby further undermined. The first serious crisis occurred early in 1968. Only with the support of a number of other OECD countries could the United States maintain the gold guarantee for a few years more.

   Parallel with this dramatic development the countries of the Group of Ten* had continued their efforts to reform the currency system. In the summer of 1967 they agreed on a procedure to create a new kind of international means of payment, the so-called Special Drawing Rights (SDR). The proposal of the Group of Ten was subsequently adopted at the annual meeting of the IMF in Rio de Janeiro in 1967. Thereby, for the first time in history, an international reserve currency was created by

* A group was formed by the ten leading OECD-countries for informal discussions about monetary issues.

a deliberate, multilateral decision. One year later the countries within the IMF decided to authorise SDRs to a value of $9.5 billions for the years 1970-72 (106).

THE DEVELOPING COUNTRIES IN THE WORLD ECONOMY

The problems of the developing countries were given only the most perfunctory attention during the international negotiations which took place during and immediately after the Second World War. This was not only due to the fact that all attention was focussed on the economic problems of Europe and the Cold War or that the majority of the present-day developing countries were then still colonies. The majority of countries and colonies in the third world had earned considerable amounts of foreign exchange by selling primary commodities during the war. India, for example, had a credit balance with British banks amounting to about $5 billions at the end of the war, and that was far more than the currency reserves of the UK (107). In the Latin American countries the industry established during the depression had been further boosted by their being shut off from former exporters during the war. The currency reserves in Latin America had risen fivefold during 1939-45 (108).

Immediately after the war a period of heavy demand also began, culminating in the military stockpiling by the United States during the Korean war. The terms of trade between primary commodities and industrial products improved by about 30 per cent and the developing countries' share of world trade rose from a quarter to a third during the period 1945-51 (109). From West Africa, for example, the export volume quadrupled during 1945-55 and the import capacity rose sixfold (110).

All this took place while the availability of investment capital was regarded as the decisive factor in the development process — an opinion that was strongly reinforced by the success of the Marshall Plan. It is not surprising, therefore, that it was to take time before the problems of the developing countries appeared on the international agenda as a matter of course.

D.C.W.E.—D

Decolonisation

At the end of the war there was no general conception that colonial liberation was around the corner (111). It is true that the United States had long before fixed a date for the independence of the Philippines. In Burma astrologers were soon at work to fix the day for national independence (112). On the Indian subcontinent the independence movement had gained such strength that it amounted to little more than the acknowledgment of a fact when Attlee announced in the spring of 1946 that the country would be granted political independence. But for the rest — and this applied mainly to the African colonies — the predominant idea was that the world would endure which, in the words of Jean Paul Sartre, 'was inhabited by two thousand millions: five hundred million people and one thousand five hundred million natives' (113). In a book published as late as 1958 the American political scientist William Y. Elliot explained that 'such areas as Nigeria and the Gold Coast, which while capable of tolerable self-rule, are certainly not proper candidates for complete independence and membership in the U.N.' (114) and Algeria could not become independent as it lacked a leader of the calibre of the Sultan of Morocco (114). De Gaulle showed himself in a speech in Brazzaville on 24 August 1958 to be a forceful proponent of assimilation and a limited autonomy rather than complete independence (115).

But the process that had begun could not be halted. Several factors made the break-up of the colonial system inevitable, even if it was not evident to contemporary observers.

Militant mass movements developed in more and more colonies. This happened first in India. It was admittedly an isolated nationalist, who wrote in Mukherjee's Magazine in 1973:

> 'Dazzled by the superficial lustre around them . . . the natives hitherto accepted the views of their superiors (and) rested their belief in them as it were in a commercial Veda. But day by day the light of intelligence is clearing up the fog in their minds' (116).

And the Indian National Congress, which was founded in 1885, was hardly more than a liberal debating club in an age when men were still impressed by colonial law and order which ensured that 'even a blind person can travel safely from Benares to Rameshwar with gold tied to a stick' (117).

But the demand of the educated upper class for gradual liberalisation was transformed in the 1920s into a radical mass movement. A similar radicalisation affected the independence movement in other Asian countries under the influence of the Russian revolutions of 1905 and 1917 and the First World War (118).

The Indian struggle for independence paved the way for national movements in other colonies. And that process which took more than half a century in India was compressed in other countries into a decade or two. This accelerated process was particularly noticeable in Africa. Kwame Nkrumah returned to the Gold Coast as Secretary General of the United Gold Coast Convention in 1948. A year later he founded a new party, won the elections of 1956 and could celebrate his country's independence as Prime Minister in the following year. The well-to-do plantation owner, Felix Houphouet-Boigny founded the Partie Democratique de Cote d'Ivoire in 1945, tactfully declined De Gaulle's offer of assimilation and emerged as leader of the independent state of the Ivory Coast in 1960. Patrice Lumumba began by demanding in the 1950s 'somewhat more liberal policies' from the Belgian colonial authorities. In 1958 he founded the Mouvement National Congolais and two years later the present-day Zaire became independent.

The demands for complete independence were the logical outcome as soon as the national movement and consciousness had acquired organised strength. The limited autonomy which had been tolerated had given rise to an educated elite which was anxious to assume sovereign power. A growing class of capitalists in the colonies began to see a brighter future in a world without colonial restrictions.

It soon became apparent also that France and Great Britain lacked the resources to hold on to colonies that were prepared to take up arms for their independence. Any remaining moral capital was lost as a result of the humiliating Suez fiasco in 1956. Only in colonies where large groups of Europeans lived did the colonial powers make serious efforts to stem the tide. But the gunboat policies of the nineteenth century turned out to be impossible in the democratic world of the postwar period. Radical groups in the mother countries protested against ruinous colonial wars and brutality. At the United Nations there was an anti-colonial bloc of socialist states and of already independent developing countries which insisted on embarrassing public debates. The United States did give financial support to the French war in Indo-China (119), but in the world of the Cold War an openly colonialist stand was impossible. At the UN the American policy was defined as an attempt to reconcile the different views of countries concerned (120).

In Africa and Asia about forty countries with a combined population of 800 million inhabitants became independent during the period 1945–60 (121). Most of the other colonies gained their independence during the 1960s. With the liberation of the former Portuguese colonies in 1975 the colonial question has been reduced, with a few exceptions, to a 'Southern Africa problem'.

The economic development of the developing countries

The new states came on the scene with a colonial inheritance that, in the words of Kwame Nkrumah, assigned to them the role of 'hewers of wood and drawers of water' (122) in a world order created by and for the rich countries (123). And during a succession of years before the great independence wave in Africa prices for primary commodities fell steeply.

This development was unavoidable, however. The postwar economic trend, followed by the Korean boom, had raised the prices for primary commodities to previously unsurpassed levels, as we have seen. A return to a more normal situation was to be expected. From 1954 to 1962 the terms of trade between primary commodities (oil being no exception) and manufactured products deteriorated by 10–15 per cent. This happened at a time when 70–90 per cent of the exports of virtually all the developing countries and colonies consisted of primary commodities and 50–60 per cent of their imports consisted of manufactured products. The exports of the developing countries during the 1950s only increased by just over 40 per cent at current prices, their share of the total world trade fell from 32 per cent to 23 per cent and a surplus in their aggregate balance of trade of $1.6 billions turned into a deficit of nearly $3 billions. These average figures give quite a reasonable picture of the development in the majority of developing countries except with regard to the balance of trade. The important oil exporters within the group of developing countries have accumulated large and growing surpluses throughout the postwar period. Developing countries within the security system of the United States could finance growing deficits during the 1950s by means of military and civilian aid. In Israel large deficits were made possible by private donations and official aid. A few other developing countries financed their deficits with income from tourists and private investment capital.

Against the background of the development outlined above, it seems remarkable that the developing countries could achieve an economic growth averaging 4.7 per cent a year during the 1950s. Even after taking into account the increase of population this implied a growth in output per capita that almost reached the level of the industrial countries, 2.4 per cent and 2.8 per cent a year respectively (124). This growth was surprisingly evenly distributed between different regions. Only in Southern Asia (India, Pakistan, Bangladesh, Burma and Sri Lanka) was it definitely below average.

In the 1960s the growth rate kept rising in most of the developing countries. The growth in output was most rapid in Eastern and Western Asia and slowest in the poor, populous states of Southern Asia and in Africa.

It is difficult to form a definite opinion about the growth of the developing countries during the 1960s as compared with earlier periods (125). It is a fairly safe guess, however, that the growth rate achieved by most developing countries both in the 1950s and in the 1960s definitely exceeded the rate of increase in production during earlier periods (126). Of the seven developing countries dealt with by Simon Kuznets in his 'Economic Growth of Nations' this guess quite clearly holds true in six cases (Mexico, Jamaica, Ghana, the Philippines, Egypt and India). Only Argentina appears to be an exception

Table 8   Annual rate of growth of GDP (1950–70) in developing and industrialised countries (volume).

		Average annual rate of growth		
		1950-60	*1961-65*	*1966-70*
All industrialised	GDP	4.0	5.2	4.6
countries	GDP per capita	2.8	3.9	3.6
All developing	GDP	4.7	5.1	5.7
countries (a)	GDP per capita	2.4	2.5	3.1
Africa	GDP	4.4	4.4	4.3
	GDP per capita	2.2	1.9	1.8
South Asia (b)	GDP	3.6	3.4	4.8
	GDP per capita	1.7	0.8	2.3
East Asia (c)	GDP	5.1	5.5	7.1
	GDP per capita	2.5	2.6	4.3
Middle East (d)	GDP	5.6	7.5	7.2
	GDP per capita	2.4	4.4	4.2
Latin America	GDP	4.9	4.9	5.7
	GDP per capita	1.9	1.9	2.6
Southern Europe (e)	GDP	5.6	7.3	6.2
	GDP per capita	4.1	5.8	4.7

(a)   Including Southern Europe (cf. note e).
(b)   Bangladesh, Burma, Ceylon, India and Pakistan.
(c)   Philippines, Hong Kong, Indonesia, Cambodia, Malaysia, Singapore, Republic of Vietnam, Taiwan and Thailand.
(d)   Iran, Iraq, Israel, Jordan, Lebanon and Syria.
(e)   Cyprus, Greece, Portugal, Spain, Turkey and Yugoslavia.

Source: IBRD Annual Reports 1968, 1971 and 1972.

Table 9   Annual rate of growth of GDP for developing countries 1900–70 (volume).

	All non-communist developing countries		Latin America		Non-communist developing countries in Asia	
	Total	*Per capita*	*Total*	*Per capita*	*Total*	*Per capita*
	%	*%*	*%*	*%*	*%*	*%*
1900–13	2.1	1.2	2.1	0.3	2.2	1.5
1913–29	1.9	0.9	2.8	1.0	1.3	0.8
1950–60	4.8	2.4	5.4	2.5	4.1	2.0
1960–70	5.1	2.4	5.5	2.5	4.8	2.1

Source: Bairoch, p. 184.

(127). On the basis of available statistics Paul Bairoch has con-
structed Table 9. It should be added, however, that Bairoch is
one of those who have doubts about UN statistics for the postwar period. Bairoch has calculated that productivity in agriculture remained practically unchanged in the 1950s and 1960s.
And the other parts of the economy can hardly have expanded
sufficiently rapidly to bring about an annual growth of GDP of
about 5 per cent (128).

The rate of increase of exports from developing countries was
more than doubled at current prices between the 1950s and the
1960s. Not even this sufficed, however, to keep pace with the
average growth of world trade. The share of the developing
countries in world exports fell a further few percentage points
to 18 per cent in 1970.

This relative decrease devolved entirely on the primary
commodity sector, which still dominated the exports of the
majority of developing countries, and there are several reasons
for this. The demand for primary commodities grew more
slowly than for manufactured products. Industrial production
was increasingly concentrated on highly processed products in
which the raw material costs are only a minor component. In
addition, raw materials were utilised more and more effectively
— less input of raw materials per manufactured unit and better
utilisation of by-products. Another reason why the position of
the developing countries *vis-a-vis* the rest of the world was so
gloomy was the emergence of the trading blocs in Europe, the
EEC and EFTA, which stimulated the internal trade between
the participating countries. While total world trade increased
fivefold at current prices during the period 1950–70, the trade
between the industrialised countries increased eightfold.

The export problem of the developing countries was, however, also due to internal factors. In most developing countries
industrialisation aimed at replacing manufactured products that
had previously been imported, so-called import substitution
(129). This required subsidies or protective tariffs for the new
industries that were established. For political, administrative
and other reasons the majority of developing countries chose
protective tariffs which were often very high. This had several
unfortunate effects. Even very inefficient industries could

develop and make good profits. Cost levels were raised throughout the economy to the disadvantage of agriculture and the
poor section of the population. Exports were hampered in both
the agricultural and the industrial sector. This policy was often
accompanied by an over-valued exchange rate (130).

Import substitution is likely to become more difficult the
longer it is pursued. Initially simple consumer goods with a mass
market can be replaced. When these possibilities have been
exhausted, the products become more complex and the home
market more restricted. But by then the policy of import substitution has already given local capitalists a strong vested
interest in maintaining status quo, which in its turn hampers the
efforts to switch to production for export.

Several researchers regard the import substitution policy as
the main reason why the exports of several developing countries
are growing relatively slowly (131). It seems doubtful whether
it has been as significant as that. During the period 1954–62 the
main explanation must have been the development of prices and
the terms of trade for primary commodities. And the relative
deterioration during the 1960s was due to the fact that the
trade between the industrialised countries grew extremely
rapidly. On the other hand, it is quite clear that the developing
countries which have increased their exports of industrial products most rapidly are those that have not adopted a pronounced
import substitution policy with the aid of tariff protection.

Critique of the existing order

The liberation movement in the developing countries had of
necessity generated promises and expectations which were out
of proportion to national resources. A demand for rapid economic growth was the obvious target and this meant, according to
all the economic experts who were hurriedly flown in from
American and European universities, that hopes of a more
equitable distribution of incomes and social reforms had to be
postponed. Growth required savings, and only the wealthy
could afford to save. The respected liberal economist Harry G.
Johnson told a Pakistani audience that 'a poor country wishing
to achieve a rapid rate of growth should not worry too much

about the distribution of resources' (132).

And this advice, which the new ruling class in many developing countries was only too willing to follow, was elevated to a national doctrine under the designation of 'functional inequality' (133).

But domestic savings were still inadequate in relation to the investment quotas calculated for the five-year plans. The initial demands of the developing countries therefore concerned aid — financial loans and grants to increase the growth rate of the economy. These demands were to a large extent met. The Colombo Plan for the Commonwealth countries was launched in 1950. Throughout the fifties aid increased rapidly. Ironically this expansion continued until the UN in 1961 adopted the so-called 1 per cent target. Thereafter the increase slowed down and finally stagnated entirely, even at current prices, for several years. In terms of fixed prices the level of aid in the mid-1970s was only slightly higher than that already reached in the 1960s (134).

The other principal demands of the developing countries concerned trade. Most of the resources, even with far more generous aid than the rich countries were capable of giving, had to be earned by exports.

The problems of the developing countries in the sphere of trade had been given some attention in GATT as early as the fifties. In concrete terms, however, this resulted primarily in allowing the developing countries to apply the trading rules fairly flexibly when it came to protecting their own home market. In 1963 GATT adopted eight recommendations as to what the industrialised countries ought to do to facilitate exports from the developing countries. Two years later a special chapter on developing countries was written into the GATT treaty. It laid down, among other things, that particular attention should be given to the export interests of the developing countries in all trade negotiations and that those countries should not be expected to reduce their tariffs in return. In the textiles sector, however, in which several developing countries were already competitive, the industrialised countries did force through restictive measures. The developing countries' exports of these goods were regulated by so-called Cotton Textiles

Agreement of 1962, later extended and prolonged (135).

The problems of the developing countries are, however, related to the main rule of GATT about non-discrimination and the way in which trade negotiations are conducted.* If a country wants to persuade other countries to lower their tariffs, it must have something to offer in return. This means that its own home market must be attractive to exporters in other countries. This is just what the majority of developing countries lack. Half of all the countries in Africa have a home market that is smaller than that of Newcastle. These countries might possibly be able to make bilateral agreements with an industrial country, but any privileges that are granted bilaterally must, according to GATT, be extended to all countries. The principle of non-discrimination thus becomes an obstacle to the attempts by the developing countries to get their needs fulfilled.

Another problem for developing countries is that even low nominal tariffs may constitute a very effective tariff protection for the industries of the industrialised countries. It is simplest to illustrate this by an example. Assume that crude copper costs $1,000 per ton and may be imported duty-free. Copper wire costs $1,200 and the duty on this product is 5 per cent or $60. The value-added is $200. This part of the production process is thus protected by a tariff of $60 or 30 per cent, and it is this effective protection that the developing countries come up against when they attempt to process their own raw materials.

This example is hypothetical but completely realistic. In his book *En ny ekonomisk världsordning* (A new international economic order) Marian Radetzki mentions that the EEC's nominal duty of 11 per cent in 1971 for vegetable oils gave effective protection of 130 per cent (136). These effects are naturally particularly great in the case of simple products, the value-added of which forms only a small part of the total costs. For more advanced industrial products like private cars, electronic products and capital goods, the effective tariffs are of no significance.

One thing industrialised countries have in common is that they import most raw materials duty-free — except competing

---

* But see pp. 57-58 for internal problems hampering the export opportunities of the developing countries.

agricultural products – but erect tariffs against processed goods. This means that they actively obstruct the attempts by the developing countries to process their own raw materials for export. And this discrimination has, if anything, increased as a result of the Kennedy Round (137).

As Table 10 shows, the tariff system of all the industrialised countries is framed in such a way that the nominal duty rises with the degree of processing. In particular the important step from raw material to semi-manufacture normally involves a sharp rise in the level of duties which, on the basis of reasonable assumptions about value-added, can be interpreted as considerable effective protection.

Table 10   Industrialised countries' average nominal tariffs for raw materials, intermediate and finished products in 1973.

	Raw materials	*Intermediate goods*	*Finished products*
	%	%	%
EEC	0.5	8.1	9.3
United States	2.7	7.6	7.9
Japan	5.9	8.6	11.2
Canada	0.3	8.4	10.2
Australia	0.9	11.1	21.0
Sweden	0.0	4.5	6.6
Austria	5.9	8.4	16.0
Switzerland	0.3	4.4	3.6
Finland	0.0	4.1	8.0
Norway	0.1	4.8	7.4
New Zealand	0.6	8.5	32.6
Average	2.0	8.0	9.8

Source: IBRD (1978), p. 58.

The developing countries' exports of processed goods, classified by material (SITC 6 leather, rubber, wood, cork and textiles, etc.), have increased more slowly than other exports of industrial goods. This is partly due to the fact that SITC 6 covers most of the products which involve a low degree of processing and are therefore affected by high effective import duties.

It was against these conditions that the developing countries launched an attack in the 1960s when they put forward the demand for preferential treatment within the international trading system — an attack on the main principles of GATT itself. The developing countries wanted the duties of the industrialised countries on imports from developing countries to be eliminated or lowered, but to be retained for imports from other countries. When the proposal was presented at the first UNCTAD conference at Geneva in 1964, the industrialised countries flatly refused even to consider it. At the following UNCTAD conference, in New Delhi in 1968, an agreement was reached, however, and at the beginning of the 1970s the industrialised countries began to give preferential treatment to imports from developing countries (the so-called General System of Preferences).

Another problem of developing countries in the sphere of trade involves the instability of export revenues. Because of large and unpredictable changes in the prices of primary commodities the developing countries find it difficult to forecast their export revenues, which makes the whole basis of economic planning unstable. The UNCTAD conference of 1964 commissioned the World Bank to study a kind of insurance scheme — supplementary financing — for the export revenues of the developing countries. This recommendation was actively sponsored by Sweden and Great Britain.

The currency questions have always been surrounded by a mystique which the experts are prone to encourage. The demands of the developing countries in the currency sphere did also remain both modest and diffuse for a long time. And even in the recommendations of the Sixth Special General Assembly of 1974 it is still not clear what is meant by 'an equitable and durable monetary system'. It is significant that Robert Solomon in his detailed and well documented study of the currency negotiations during the postwar period, 'The International Monetary System 1945-1976 — an Insider's View', hardly mentions the developing countries (138). Even when the IMF had begun to function according to its original intentions the real negotiations took place within the exclusive Group of 10, the members of which were the ten leading industrial nations of the world. It was this group that, in splendid isolation, elaborated the proposals for reforms which the IMF later adopted, including the SDR reform.

Poor and less poor developing countries

It has always been a customary proviso to note that the developing countries are not really a homogenous group. Books and lectures on the developing countries often devote an introductory section to explain that there are differences between India and the Maldives as well as between Libya and Papua New Guinea. This is often followed by a discussion which leads to the conclusion that there are nevertheless so many similarities that it is permissible to generalise for the whole — or at least almost the whole — group of developing countries (139). And the reason is obviously that it is impossible to deal with developments in 120–130 countries without generalising.

Whether this is acceptable or not obviously depends on the object in view. There are undoubtedly a number of spheres, e.g. infant mortality, productivity in agriculture, literacy and physical infrastructure — where the differences are quite palpable between, on the one hand, virtually all the developing countries and, on the other, nearly all the OECD countries. Even an occasional visitor in the countryside can usually decide whether he is in a developing or an industrialised country without the aid of climate and the colour of people's skin. In other spheres the differences are less clear or completely obliterated. There are, for example, several developing countries which have a higher proportion of manufactured products in their exports than many industrialised countries.

The interesting thing, however, is the difference within the group that has jointly demanded a new world order. During the 1960s it began to be apparent that development in all fields was much faster in the somewhat wealthier developing countries than in the very poorest. These trends have strengthened during the 1970s.

This pattern is very clear in Tables 11 and 12. The aggregate output in all developing countries increased during the periods 1960–70 and 1970–77 by, on average 5–6 per cent a year. Most rapid of all was the growth of GDP in the oil exporting developing countries and in those with rapidly growing exports of industrial products. Among the other developing countries, the GDP increased most rapidly in the wealthiest and most slowly

Table 11 Population, Gross Domestic Product (GDP) and GDP growth rate 1960–77 for developing countries classified by major export and income category.

	Periods	All developing countries	Major petroleum exporters	Other developing countries — Total	Fast growing exporters of manufactures	29 least developed countries	Remaining countries	Classified according to GDP per capita in 1976 — Over $800	$400–$800	Under $400
Population (millions)	1976	1,969	308	1,662	240	250	1,172	404	293	1,273
Population (per square kilometer)	1976	29	22	31	18	19	43	14	26	47
Gross Domestic Product (millions of US $)	1976	1,014,544	295,356	719,188	35,014	35,014	372,434	614,215	167,043	232,286
GDP/capita (US $)	1976	515	960	433	1,300	140	318	1,523	571	182
Annual rate of growth of GDP	1960–70	5.3%	6.3%	5.2%	6.2%	3.1%	4.7%	6.2%	5.5%	4.1%
	1970–77	5.8%	8.1%	5.3%	7.1%	3.2%	4.2%	6.8%	6.5%	3.6%
GDP/capita	1960–70	2.8%	3.7%	2.6%	3.3%	0.8%	2.2%	3.4%	2.7%	1.6%
	1970–77	3.2%	5.3%	2.8%	4.4%	0.7%	1.8%	4.0%	3.7%	1.2%

Source: UNCTAD (1979), p. 480.

* Algeria, Angola, Bahrain, Brunei, Ecuador, Gabon, Indonesia, Iran, Iraq, Kuwait, Libya, Nigeria, Oman, Qatar, Saudi Arabia, Trinidad and Tobago, United Arab Emirates and Venezuela.
** Argentina, Brazil, Hong Kong, Mexico, Republic of Korea and Singapore.

Table 12 Exports: Annual average growth rates 1950–78 for developing countries by major export and income category.

Periods	All developing countries	Major petroleum exporters*	Total	Other developing countries Fast growing exporters of manufactures**	29 least developed	Remaining countries	Classified according to GDP per capita in 1976 Over $800	$800–400	Under $400
	%	%	%	%	%	%	%	%	%
1950–60	2.9	7.5	1.4	– 0.3	2.7	2.0	3.6	4.0	1.0
1960–70	6.9	7.7	6.5	7.6	4.5	6.3	7.5	8.1	4.1
1970–78	23.9	30.0	18.9	22.1	11.3	17.7	25.9	21.0	17.9

Source: UNCTAD (1979), p. 35.

* Cf. corresponding note in Table 11.
** Cf. corresponding note in Table 11.

in the very poorest. As the population growth was most rapid in the latter countries, the differences in GDP per inhabitant become even more pronounced. During the 1960s, output per capita in the majority of the poorest countries increased by 1-2 per cent, only to decline somewhat during the seventies. In the middle income countries (GDP/inhabitant $400–800) the increase was almost twice as rapid during the sixties and three times as rapid during the seventies. And the distance to the wealthy developing countries was even greater.

On the trading side the picture is the same. The wealthy countries have since the early sixties been able to increase their export revenues far more quickly than the very poorest. Table 12 also shows that these differences between various groups of developing countries were not at all in evidence during the 1950s. We have pointed out earlier that the growth in GNP was relatively similar in various regions of the developing world during the 1950s. In the case of exports there was then no uniform pattern of any kind which can be related to differences in income.

These large — and in most cases growing — differences between various groups of developing countries during the last 15-20 years can be seen in practically every sphere. The most serious thing may be that productivity in agriculture has increased very slowly in several of the poorest countries, which has made them more and more dependent on imports. In the mid-1960s the United States shipped about 800,000 tons of grain a month to India alone. This was enough to provide for 40 million people, which was about the number of inhabitants in the coastal cities of India (140). The very large-scale food aid given to the developing countries has in many cases been necessary to alleviate distress and starvation. But the long-term effects are probably negative. Low, stable prices and large-scale food aid must have in all probability hampered domestic output. The crisis came in the 1970s when crop failures and large-scale Russian purchases on the international market raised prices to record levels — at the same time as the food aid ceased. Previously, this form of aid had quite simply been a method of disposing of an embarrassing surplus (141). When the prospects for commercial sales brightened, the aid ceased.

Of all sectors agriculture is the one in which the most adverse change for the developing countries has occurred during the postwar period. Before the Second World War the developing countries had a grain surplus for export amounting to 7 per cent of the total output. By 1972 this had been transformed into a deficit of 8 per cent (142). And it is obviously in the poorest countries, with a slow growth of exports, that this situation has serious repercussions.

Table 13   Food production per capita 1961–76 (Index 1961–65 = 100).

	1961	1966	1970	1971	1972	1973	1974	1975	1976
Industrialised countries	96	104	107	113	111	113	115	118	119
Developing countries	100	97	104	102	99	100	100	103	105
Latin America	100	101	106	103	101	101	103	103	108
Middle East	97	101	103	103	107	99	105	109	111
South and South-east Asia	101	94	105	103	97	104	99	106	105
Africa	97	96	100	99	95	89	93	93	94
Eastern Europe	99	114	117	117	114	133	125	117	129
Centrally planned countries in Asia	96	103	108	110	107	110	110	112	112

Source: UNCTAD (1977), Table 6.5A, pp. 242–43.

An important cause of the situation of the poorest countries — and in particular of the worsened situation in the 1970s — is the evolution for the purchasing power of exports.

Table 14 shows changes in the purchasing power of exports for various groups of developing countries, i.e. taking into account both the price and volume changes for exports and prices for imports.* All countries, except the major oil exporters have seen their terms of trade deteriorate during the seventies. The somewhat wealthier developing countries have been able to compensate for an unfavourable development of the terms of trade by increasing exports, while the purchasing power of the least developed countries has fallen by about 15 per cent during the 1970s. (143)

* Purchasing power of exports is defined as value index for exports deflated by unit value of imports.

Table 14 Purchasing power of exports: developing countries by major export and income groups (Index 1970 = 100)

	1960	1965	1970	1971	1972	1973	1974	1975	1976	1977	1978
All developing countries	58	72	100	104	114	137	199	176	211	220	204
Major petroleum exporters	54	73	100	121	130	163	374	318	382	380	323
Other developing countries	59	72	100	95	105	124	123	113	134	145	148
Of which:											
Fast growing exporters of manufactures	51	63	100	101	119	153	139	129	162	184	201
29 least developed countries	70	85	100	88	91	85	76	70	87	97	84
Remaining countries	59	73	100	93	100	113	116	108	122	129	128
Of which:											
Countries with a per capita GNP in 1976											
over $800	52	66	100	109	118	146	231	208	249	255	235
$400–$800	48	68	100	98	111	133	160	141	166	180	172
Less than $400	73	82	100	93	100	109	118	106	125	138	130

Source: UNCTAD (1979), Table 2.6, p. 63.

There is in fact only one sphere in which the position of the poorest developing countries is more favourable than that of the wealthier countries in the third world. That relates to the burden of debts. Developing countries with a GNP per inhabitant of less than $200 in 1974 pay about one tenth of the aggregate interest and debt repayments of the whole group of developing countries, but their share of production is clearly larger (144).

This impressionistic picture of the difference in economic terms between various groups of developing countries suffices to allow certain important conclusions. When it comes to economic development one cannot talk about developing countries in general. The growing gap — which plays such a central role in the debate about the developing countries — does not run between industrialised countries and developing countries. It runs between the billion people who live in the poorest countries on earth and the rest of the world. That is not to say that there are no people living in poverty both in industrialised countries and in the somewhat wealthier developing countries. But one can never escape the fact that the resources to satisfy people's needs are incomparably smaller in the poorest countries.

The question of an equitable distribution of the world's resources applies not to countries, however, but to people (145). During the 1960s, several developing countries reached the growth targets that had been set. But only a small number of countries managed to give the broad masses of people a share of the increased resources. In the majority of developing countries there was a decline in the proportion of incomes and wealth going to the worst situated groups. Several researchers even argue that the situation deteriorated in absolute terms for the poor in many countries.

And the main reason for this is political. The tax systems in most developing countries lack any element of progressivity; in many cases they are regressive. Taxation of landownership and other wealth is rare. The expenditure side of the budget is often dominated by investments and subsidies that favour small elites. The owners of capital also receive support from effective tariffs which in several cases are measured in percentages that run into hundreds. This enables even inefficient enterprises to take in considerable profits.* Local government investments and other infrastructure at best favour the middle class as well as the upper class. The attempts to speed up industrial investments have also resulted in developing countries outbidding each other in offering tax concessions to transnational enterprises.

This inexcusably brief and simplified picture is unfortunately true for the majority of developing countries today — as also for many industrialised countries several decades after the democratic breakthrough. The critique also puts in perspective the tremendous performances, both past and present, in those developing countries that have seriously attempted to achieve — and in some cases have succeeded in achieving — a more even distribution of productive resources and power.

It is thus not the case, as is often maintained in the debate about development, that a lop-sided distribution is a necessary or automatic result of the growth or development process. It is, instead, a logical consequence of a growth that

> 'takes place in a society in which the economic and social structure is inequitable; in which all the mechanisms of power are designed to give more to those who already have. It is important to make clear that it is not only a matter of interaction between growth and a distribution of wealth that is lop-sided from the start. The owners of capital and land in several cases hold both the actual and formal power in society. It is this that explains why positive government measures in so many developing countries reinforce the development toward greater differences of income and wealth' (146).

We shall return to the question raised by this development. How is the 'national order' affected by changes at the international level? And which order — the national or the international — is most important from the point of view of global equity?

---

* See the earlier section on import substitution policy.

The threat from the developing countries

There is another reason to take account of the important differences between various developing countries. Only a few years ago the meaning of 'problems of the developing countries' was unambiguous. But today there are two debates about the developing countries. One concerns starvation, lack of resources, aid and development problems in the poor countries. The other concerns the growing competition from a number of rapidly expanding exporters of industrial products — a group of countries which have already been provided with an acronym — NIC (Newly Industrializing Countries).

Exports of industrial products from the whole group of developing countries increased more rapidly during the 1960s and 1970s than those of the OECD countries. During the period 1960-75 exports of manufactured goods from the developing countries was increased by 12.3 per cent at fixed prices compared to 8.8 per cent for industrialised countries (see Table 19), and the difference has grown larger during the seventies.

The developing countries still sell mainly light consumer goods on the international market, e.g. textiles and readymade clothing, wood and leather products, sports articles, processed agricultural products, toys and electrical equipment. Eleven developing countries — Argentina, Brazil, Egypt, Hong Kong, India, Israel, Mexico, Pakistan, Singapore, South Korea and Taiwan — together account for about 75 per cent of the aggregate export of manufactured goods from the developing countries. But both the number of commodity groups and of exporters is steadily growing.

In the case of more advanced industrial products the developing countries' share of world trade is small but their exports are rapidly increasing. Thus throughout the 1960s the developing countries' group expanded their export of machinery and transport equipment by almost 20 per cent a year. For certain limited commodity groups an annual expansion rate of more than 30 per cent was recorded (147). The percentage rate of increase will decline. But if one looks at the absolute effect, it is rather a process that has only just begun.

There are many features of this development which deserve

closer study. It is clear, for instance, that the transnational corporations have to a large extent farmed out labour-intensive stages of production to developing countries.

Thus US-owned transnational corporations accounted for 40 per cent of the export of industrial products from Latin America in 1968 (148). In Brazil foreign capital controlled 70 per cent of the 679 largest enterprises in the country at the beginning of the 1970s (149). The successful electronics industry in Singapore, which was established within a few years (1968–71), is dominated by transnational corporations and is to a large degree geared to the export of components to the parent companies (150). In countries like Hong Kong, Taiwan, South Korea and Columbia, Sanjaya Lall and Paul Streeten reckon that transnational corporations account for 15–30 per cent of exports (151). A more important factor is probably the sub-contracting of production to nationally owned enterprises by the international corporations. Kathryn Morton and Peter Tulloch estimate, on admittedly shaky grounds, that while transnational corporations account directly for 10 per cent of Asian developing countries' exports of manufactured goods, they account as buyers for 50–80 per cent through various production contracts (152). The sub-contracting by transnational corporations of the production of manufactured goods in developing countries has probably increased in recent years. On the other hand, the share of developing countries' exports which is handled by foreign-owned enterprises appears to have remained unchanged or to have slightly diminished since the mid-1960s (153).

In several developing countries domestic capital both private and public, plays a growing part in the export industry. And some developing countries, e.g. Brazil, have begun to be able to take a firm stand in negotiations with the big corporations. It is of course important to form an opinion about what the longer-term political and social consequences of the rapid industrialisation in the developing countries are likely to be (154).

These questions cannot be treated here as adequately as they deserve. We shall confine ourselves to noting that competition from the developing countries will not in future be a matter only of clothes and toys. Iron ore extraction is far cheaper in several developing countries today than in Sweden. The steelworks being planned and built today in the developing countries will probably be able to sell commercial steel at prices that will not cover the costs in this country. The position of the NIC's *vis-a-vis* the 'old' industrialised countries as regards conditions for industrial production will continue to improve in *all* respects with the probable exception of the wage level.

The threatening picture could be extended. But in observing the rapid change in the exports of industrial commodities from several developing countries it is important to remember that their absolute significance is still minimal. Throughout the 1960s industrial products from the developing countries formed about 6 per cent of the total imports of the rich countries. By 1975 the share had increased to nearly 9 per cent. Calculated as a proportion of the total consumption in the industrialised countries the imports of manufactured goods from developing countries constituted less than 1 per cent during the 1960s and 1.2 per cent in 1975. The World Bank has made a forecast indicating that this share will amount to 2.7 per cent by 1985 (155).

Table 15   Annual growth of the volume of exports 1960–75

	Total world trade %	Industrialised countries %	Developing countries %
Food	4.1	5.2	2.8
Other agricultural raw materials	4.5	5.6	2.6
Non-fuel minerals and metals	3.9	3.1	4.8
Fuel and energy	6.3	4.2	6.2
Manufactures	8.8	8.8	12.3
Total merchandise	7.1	7.5	5.9

Source: IBRD (1978), p. 27.

It is also important to emphasize that the industrialisation of the developing countries does not only lead to increased competition but also to greater exports from OECD countries – at least in a medium-term perspective. During the period 1974–78 the oil-importing developing countries have financed an aggregate deficit in the balance of trade of more than $160 billions, corresponding to 20–30 per cent of their imports (156). In this way they have made a valuable contribution to the efforts to mitigate the recession.*

The really serious situation, paradoxically enough, arises when the developing countries begin to repay their loans. They will then have to produce an export surplus — in other words, sell more to 'us' than we sell to 'them' — in order to save enough money for interest and loan repayments. And this development has already begun in Taiwan — one of the most successful of the new industrial countries. Between 1974-75 and 1976-77 a deficit in the balance of trade of about $1 billion a year was turned into a surplus of $0.5-1 billion (157). And in 1978 a substantial surplus was recorded. Also a number of other NIC's seem to be moving towards a positive trade balance.

Instead of today's aggregate deficit of $20-30 billions a year for oil-importing developing countries we must posit a future surplus of perhaps $15-20 billions. For those receiving these billions life should not hold any problems. But what will happen to employment when the world market potential for the industrialised countries shrinks by $40-50 billions or about 3-4 per cent of the total world exports of today? In theory there are elegant solutions, but the question is whether they can be applied in practice.

A WORLD ORDER IN CRISIS

The British historian E. J. Hobsbawn has characterised the period that began after the revolutions of 1848 and ended in the depression of the 1870s as the golden age of economic liberalism. Maybe the 1960s will one day be remembered in the same vein.

The trading system was liberalised in the sixties and prepared the way for a rapid and stable increase in international commodity exchange and production. Currencies were convertible and exchange rates fixed. The price ratio between raw materials and manufactured goods was stabilised. The developing countries were granted preferences within a preserved GATT system. The currency system was provided with a mechanism to create international liquidity in step with the needs of world trade.

* See further p. 76.

The big corporations regained faith in the stability of the world economy and the private capital flows increased rapidly.

The future appeared bright and the problems seemed manageable at the beginning of the 1970s, as they had a century earlier. But perhaps the 1960s, like the decades around the middle of the nineteenth century, were 'a rather special interlude' (158).

The dynamic free trade era around the middle of the nineteenth century passed over in 1873 into the longest depression in history. The golden 1960s ended in the crisis of 1973, and was not only a matter of oil.

The system of fixed exchange rates finally broke down. The governments in the industrialised countries began to lose control over inflation. In the summer of 1973 the United States imposed an embargo on the export of forty different agricultural products and scrap metal. Protectionist tendencies became increasingly evident. OPEC quadrupled the price of oil and prohibited exports to the United States and the Netherlands. Unemployment reached a level reminiscent of the 1930s.

The symptoms of a crisis in the old economic world order were obvious and no new order was in sight. Secretary of State Kissinger's proposal for a new Atlantic Charter was coldly received in Europe. The world was no longer the same — the harmony of the Congress of Vienna could not be recreated.

The seventies began with an unusually intensive and simultaneous trade boom in most countries of the world. Raw material prices began to rise steeply in 1971–1972 and accelerated during 1973. In several branches production reached the limit of its capacity (159). For many developing countries it proved impossible to obtain a number of investment and consumer goods such as pipes for irrigation plant and newsprint.

This trade boom had already passed its peak when the OPEC states quadrupled the price of oil, a purchase tax in the order of $75 billions on the energy consumption of the rest of the world or about 2 per cent of the GDP of the OECD countries. This accelerated the decline of trade at the same time as the balance of trade was seriously weakened in virtually all oil-importing countries. Economic policies fell out of rhythm. Several industrialised countries concentrated on maintaining employment and allowed the trade balance deficits to grow. Other countries took immediate steps to fight inflation, which continued despite the decline in trade and gave economists a new object for study — stagflation. These countries allowed unemployment to reach record levels in their effort to protect the external balance. By means of a restrictive economic policy West Germany managed to greatly increase its trade balance surplus. The OPEC states could not avoid accumulating enormous trade balance surpluses. And forecasts were immediately made of enormous surpluses that indicated a very gloomy future for the wealthy countries.

Table 16   Annual rate of growth of GDP 1970–77.

	1970–73	1973–74	1974–75	1975–76	1976–77
	%	%	%	%	%
Developed countries	5.1	0.3	−0.6	5.2	3.7
EEC	4.4	1.7	−1.8	5.0	2.2
United States	4.7	−1.3	−1.0	5.8	4.9
Japan	8.7	−1.0	2.4	6.0	5.1
Developing countries	6.3	6.0	4.4	5.6	5.7
Latin America	7.4	7.2	3.2	4.9	4.6
Africa	5.0	5.5	2.7	5.4	4.1
Middle East	10.0	9.4	5.8	10.0	8.8
South and South-east Asia	4.2	3.2	6.6	5.1	7.0
Eastern Europe	6.6	6.0	5.4	5.4	4.9

Source: UNCTAD Handbook (1979), Table 6.2, pp. 482–486.

Several oil-importing developing countries (see the 15 selected countries in Table 17) and the countries of Southern Europe decided on a policy of continued expansion. They were given more aid, borrowed the rest and continued to increase their imports from the wealthy countries. During the two years 1974–75 alone these twenty countries* are reckoned to have financed a trade deficit with over $80 borrowed billions. The increased imports which were financed in this way corresponded to 4–5 per cent of all world exports during those years.

It was quite simply these countries that made the most important contribution to overcome the crisis in the wealthy countries. The additional demand generated by them in the OECD countries must have corresponded to over 2 million jobs.

---

* Fifteen selected developing countries in Table 17 together with the five countries of Southern Europe in the same table.

Table 17 Trade balance 1970–75 for selected countries and groups of countries (value in billions of dollars).

	1970	1971	1972	1973	1974	1975	1976	1977	1978
United States	+ 2.8	−2.0	−6.3	+ 1.6	−10.0	+ 3.2	−15.5	−37.7	−41.6
France	−1.2	−0.7	−0.8	−1.4	−7.1	−2.0	−8.6	−6.9	−5.4
Italy	−1.8	−0.9	−0.7	−5.7	−10.6	−3.5	−6.5	−2.5	−1.2
Great Britain	−2.3	−1.5	−3.5	−8.3	−15.5	−9.4	−9.7	−6.1	−1.8
EFTA	−4.5	−4.8	−4.6	−5.7	−10.8	−9.4	−10.7	−12.6	−6.2
Southern Europe*	−5.2	−5.3	−6.1	−8.9	−16.5	−18.5	−17.7	−20.0	−15.7
Federal Republic of Germany	+ 4.4	+ 4.7	+ 6.4	+ 12.9	+ 20.2	+ 15.8	+ 14.3	+ 17.2	+ 21.2
Japan	+ 0.4	+ 4.3	+ 5.1	−1.3	−6.4	−2.0	+ 2.4	+ 9.8	+ 18.3
Oil exporting developing countries	+ 6.5	+ 9.3	+ 9.9	+ 16.9	+ 88.4	+ 60.4	+ 76.4	+ 67.5	+ 47.8
Non-oil exporting developing countries	−8.7	−13.3	−11.5	−12.2	−30.5	−41.5	−24.3	−25.3	−40.0
15 selected countries**	−4.9	−6.7	−5.7	−7.5	−22.5	−28.0	−19.2	−18.5	−23.7
Eastern Europe	−0.7	−0.6	−2.3	−3.3	−5.4	−13.9	−11.5	−6.5	−8.0

Source: UNCTAD Handbook, Supplement 1977, Tables 1.11 and 1.12, pp. 26–34; Handbook 1979, Table 1.11, pp. 42–51.

* Greece, Spain, Turkey, Yugoslavia and Gibraltar
** Brazil, Mexico, Peru, Panama, Morocco, Egypt, the Sudan, Yemen, the Philippines, Singapore, Thailand, Republic of Korea, Pakistan, India and Israel.

The expansive developing countries succeeded, like the countries in Southern Europe, in maintaining a relatively high rate of growth by borrowing money for imports. At the same time, however, they increased their foreign debts far faster than their repayment capacity. Several of these countries now have to devote over a quarter of their export revenues to interest and loan repayments. The main cause of the growing deficits of these countries is not increased oil prices. According to one study, 55 per cent of the weakening of the balance of trade in 1973-74, and 75 per cent of the deterioration in 1974-75, can be attributed to the recession in the industrialised countries (160). And it is only through an increased rate of expansion in the OECD countries that these countries can solve their debt problems.

Paradoxically, however, these large debts are also a means of power. The international banks are so heavily involved in these countries that they can hardly withdraw. By the end of 1976 non-OPEC developing countries owed private banks about $75 billions. Around $45 billions of these debts were due to American banks. The banks simply had to grant new loans in order to get the old ones repaid (161). And the OECD countries cannot cease to give aid and export credits. Should they do so the heavily indebted countries would be forced to reduce imports and go all out for exports. But the question is whether the industrialised countries can afford to dispense with the expanding market offered by these countries.

The situation indicates a new theme in the international negotiations of the 1970s — the common interest between rich countries with saturated markets and poor expanding developing countries. Is there a common interest that can be institutionalised as a cohesive force in a new international economic order? And if so, what will the position of the least developed countries be in that order?

The first acute dollar crisis occurred, as we have said, in 1968. Thanks to rescue actions by the leading industrial countries the currency system was patched together in a tolerable way. The United States' balance of payments was stabilised in 1968-69, but in 1970 there was a new record deficit of nearly $10 billions and during the first nine months of 1971 the

United States' 'debts to foreign currency authorities' grew by more than $21 billions. The situation became untenable and in August 1971 President Nixon announced that the dollar could no longer be converted into gold (162).

A new attempt to maintain a system of fixed exchange rates was made by means of the so-called Smithsonian Accord in December 1971 when the dollar was devalued and the yen, Deutsche mark and Swiss franc were revalued against other currencies.

The forces that were at play could not be harnessed, however, by agreements and sacred promises by finance ministers. The dollar drain from the United States amounted to $50 billions in 1970–72 (163). A currency system with fixed exchange rates presupposes that countries are in relatively similar economic situations – above all with regard to domestic inflation and the raising of productivity. But international inflation – which according to Marina Whitman is 'a painful phenomenon in search of a theory' (164) – assumed quite different forms in the leading currency countries. And the financial and credit policies of these countries were not likely to strengthen confidence in the exchange rates of the Smithsonian Accord. International currency speculators had enormous sums at their disposal with which to fulfill their own prophecies about the weakness of any given currency.

The system collapsed in February–March 1973. The industrial countries decided to let their currencies float freely or locked to various regional arrangements. By then the work to reform the international monetary system had already started in IMF's Committee of Twenty. This group attempted to devise procedures to guide the adjustment process and to find an appropriate form to settle the existing imbalances within a new monetary order where SDRs were supposed to be the principal reserve asset. No agreement could however be reached about the 'Outline of Reform' presented by the Committee. And the negotiations which continued in the Interim Committee only confirmed the lack of consensus. One could argue that this committee, at its fifth meeting in Jamaica in January 1976, formally acknowledged the breakdown of the Bretton Woods system. With regard to exchange rate regimes, settlement of official balances and the reserve system the Jamaica Agreement simply recognizes the emerging monetary disorder and allows member countries to solve their problems to the best of their ability.

Oil crisis, galloping inflation, deep recession, record unemployment, menacing protectionism and the old currency system in ruins, it was at this juncture — marked by uncertainty and gloomy prophecies about the future of democracy — that the developing countries put forward their proposal for a new international economic order.

Notes

1. Kenwood & Lougheed, p. 91. The figures refer to imports and exports in relation to total output.
2. Ibid., p. 22.
3. Bunte & Jorberg, p. 22.
4. Weber, p. 207.
5. Bunte & Jorberg, p. 24.
6. Mauro, p. 152.
7. Hughes, p. 153.
8. Bunte & Jorberg, p. 18.
9. Gould discusses in detail various calculations of the significance of technology or the so-called residual factor (p. 295 et seq.).
10. Condliffe, p. 206.
11. Kenwood & Lougheed, pp. 33–34; Dillard, p. 535; Hughes, p. 144.
12. Kenwood & Lougheed, p. 34.
13. Kenwood & Lougheed give the figure of 3 per cent, while Gould, for example, believes it to be closer to later calculations which put it no higher than 1.7 per cent.
14. Kenwood & Lougheed. p. 34; Hughes, p. 144.
15. See, for example, the calculations of Kuznets (1971) for Argentina, Mexico, Jamaica, Ghana, the Philippines, Egypt and India.
16. Kuznets (1966), pp. 312-13.
17. Yates, pp. 32-33; Kenwood & Lougheed, p. 93.
18. According to the Brussels definition, which puts the share of raw materials a few percentage points higher than if the Standard International Trade Classification (SITC) had been used.
19. Ferry; extract in Fieldhouse (1967), p. 52.
20. Szentes, p. 135.
21. Panikkar, pp. 32–33. It is remarkable how all the 'great deeds' portrayed in our school-books are European deeds.
22. McNeill, pp. 203-32.
23. An excellent analysis of the classical economists' view of colonies is to be found in Winch.

24. Fieldhouse (1971), p. 179.
25. Hopkins, pp. 91–102. The slave trade was banned in most European countries during the first half of the nineteenth century and the volume declined rapidly from the 1830s. The export of slaves was fairly quickly replaced to some by exportation of palm oils and groundnuts.
26. Fieldhouse (1971), p. 18; Mauro, p. 225 et seq.
27. Mill, extract in Fieldhouse (1967), p. 34. One must remember that economists of that period regarded 'the iron law of wages' or, in Mill's case, the 'wage fund theory' as axiomatic. Economics was a zero sum game. Higher wages immediately reduced profits.
28. A detailed and well documented account of the attitudes within the ruling groups in Great Britain and Germany is given in James and Stern.
29. Fieldhouse (1971), p. 213.
30. Hobsbawn (1969), p. 146.
31. James, p. 32 et seq.
32. op cit., pp. 81–93. The Home Rule crisis lasted from 8 June 1885 to 8 June 1886. The annexation took place in December 1885.
33. Richard Cobden: 'How wars are got up in India', quoted in Pannikkar, p. 107. Peripheral developments as a central explanation of imperialism is the main thesis of the extensive works on colonial policy by the British historian D. K. Fieldhouse. See in particular Fieldhouse (1971) and (1973).
34. The 'imperialism' debate has curiously enough come to focus on the thesis that colonies were economically necessary. This is not very fruitful. In order to explain the process it is enough to examine whether ruling elites regarded colonies as being of sufficient advantage to their own interests, which were identified with those of the nation. Such judgements were based on the prevailing economic doctrine and the experiences of earlier colonial acquisitions. The Eldorado of the Spaniards still lived on in the dreams of the nineteenth century. One should probably also distinguish between the original reasons for annexing colonies and the factors which led to the expansion of such possessions.
35. The dividends of the Compagnie Francaise de l'Afrique Occidentale never fell below 20 per cent during 1912–19. British Malacca Rubber Plantations Ltd yielded 10–75 per cent in the same period. The gold mines gave an average of 8 per cent. The interest rate in Europe was at that time 3–5 per cent. It should, however, be added that quite a few companies were unprofitable. (Fieldhouse (1971), pp. 387–89.)
36. Fieldhouse (1971), pp. 147–48.
37. Between 1831 and 1877, through the so-called Culture System (taxation of agricultural production in certain regions) the Dutch treasury received 823 million guilders around 18 millions a year, while at the same time the Netherlands' state budget amounted to 60 millions. (Fieldhouse (1971), pp. 332–33.)
38. Hopkins. It was partly the concern to eliminate the African middlemen which led to annexations by France in West Africa (Hopkins, p. 156). Wolff, pp. 97–193.
39. Maddison (1971), p. 13 et seq.
40. An interesting and well documented description of ecologically balanced societies in developing countries is provided in Wilkinson, chap. 3–4.
41. Kenwood & Lougheed, pp. 38–40; Robinson, pp. 5–6.
42. Sodersten, p. 129.
43. op. cit., pp. 122–29.

44. op. cit., p. 129.
45. Maddison (1971), pp. 64–65.
46. Saul, p. 62.
47. Hobsbawn (1969), p. 149. It was thus 'savings' in China which were 'the key to Britain's whole payments pattern'.
48. Fieldhouse (1973), pp. 152–53.
49. op. cit., pp. 55–59.
50. Kenwood & Lougheed, pp. 38–47.
51. Kuznets (1966), pp. 312–314.
52. Kuznets (1966), p. 475.
53. Guano consisted of bird droppings and fish remnants. It was collected from the breeding grounds of marine birds and used as fertilizer in agriculture.
54. Kindleberger, p. 76.
55. Bairoch, pp. 162–63.
56. Bairoch, pp. 57–58.
57. Kuznets (1965), pp. 177–78; Kuznets (1971), p. 24.
58. Condliffe, pp. 444–45.
59. Condliffe, p. 456.
60. Routh, pp. 263–71.
61. Condliffe, p. 456.
62. The figure is uncertain due to difficulties in comparing Soviet statistics with those of other countries. The correctness of the report has been strongly questioned by several researchers. See e.g. Harris, pp. 213–46.
63. Blum, p. 91 et seq.
64. Wilkins (1965), p. 252. How profitable this market was is shown, for instance, by Vaitsos, p. 62 et seq., and Ledogar.
65. Ashworth, p. 260.
66. Solomon, p. 14.
67. Hudson (1972), p. XVII and 35 et seq.
68. Ashworth, p. 259.
69. Ashworth, p. 259; Hudson (1972), p. 37; Condliffe, p. 531 et seq.; Kenwood & Lougheed, p. 252.
70. Kolko (1970), p. 490.
71. Kolko (1970), p. 247 et seq.
72. Kolko (1970), pp. 252–53. A higher estimate set the requirement at $14 billions.
73. Hearings of the House Special Committee on Postwar Policy and Planning, 78th Congress, 2nd Session 1944, p. 1082. Quoted in Weissman, p. 38.
74. Lary, p. 13.
75. Quotation in Kolko (1970), pp. 249–50.
76. Ashworth, p. 268; Hughes, p. 273.
77. Quoted in Kolko (1970), p. 251. Kolko's work provides a very detailed and well documented account of how the postwar plans of the United States developed.
78. Ellsworth, p. 512.
79. A good description of the origin of GATT and the way it operates is to be found in Gardner.
80. Sodersten, p. 392.
81. Quotations in Blum, p. 308.
82. Mason & Asher, p. 12. This 900-page volume must be regarded as the standard work on the origin and development of the World Bank.
83. Solomon, pp. 12–13.

84. Quoted in Mason & Asher, p. 2.
85. Mason & Asher, p. 105.
86. Mason & Asher, p. 125.
87. Quoted in Condliffe, p. 657.
88. A brief description of the various phases on the way to full convertibility is to be found in Tew.
89. Solomon, p. 31.
90. Fortune, February 1961, p. 222.
91. Blum, pp. 306–307. The Southern and Western farm bloc in Congress even managed to tie part of UNRRA's resources to purchases of American agricultural products, especially wool and cotton.
92. Hughes, p. 266.
93. Dillard, pp. 538–39.
94. *The Times History of Our Times.* It is significant that Canada's contributions are overlooked in nearly all the historical literature. Already during the war Canada gave more so-called lend-lease aid per inhabitant than the United States.
95. Tew, p. 38.
96. Solomon, p. 21.
97. UNCTAD (1976), p. 341.
98. Wilkins (1975), pp. 283 and 375. Wilkins (1970) and (1975) presumably provides the best, even if somewhat uncritical account of the overseas establishments of the large American enterprises.
99. Japan's foreign investments increased fifteenfold during the period 1960–71 at current prices. During the following five years their book value increased from $4.4 billions to $19.4 billions. Japan and West Germany each controlled 7 per cent of the private investments in the OECD countries in 1976. Statistical information about the investments of transnational enterprises can be found in United Nations (1973) and (1978).
100. United Nations (1973), p. 18. This conclusion is in the main confirmed in United Nations (1978).
101. Lall & Streeten, p. 15.
102. Internationella koncerner i industrilander. SOU 1975: 50, p. 83.
103. op. cit., p. 35.
104. Solomon, pp. 19–20.
105. Machlup, pp. 147–49.
106. The creation of SDRs is simply a book-keeping transaction. Each country in the IMF is credited at a given point in time with a certain amount of SDRs. These are included in that country's currency reserve and may be used as international means of payment according to certain rules. Their distribution among the member countries in the IMF corresponds to the size of their quotas. The wealthy countries therefore receive most. This circumstance would soon be taken by the developing countries as a justification for proposing a so-called link between SDRs and aid. The aim of this proposal was simply that the SDRs that were created should primarily be distributed, directly or by other means, among the developing countries.
107. Haellkvist & Sanden-Haellkvist, p. 122; Maddison (1971), p. 66.
108. United Nations, February 1949, p. 114; Halperin in Petras & Zeitlin, pp. 44–46.
109. IBRD (1973).
110. Hopkins, p. 267.
111. Tucker, p. 31.

112. *Ansprenger*, p. 176.

113. Sartre in the preface to Frantz Fanon's book *The Wretched of the Earth*.

114. Elliott in 'Strausz-Hupe & Hazard', pp. 439–40. See also Perham. It should be noted that the Gold Coast became the independent state of Ghana a year before Elliott's essay was published.

115. Quoted in *Ansprenger*, p. 257.

116. Quoted in Hobsbawn (1975), p. 123.

117. Hobsbawn (1975), p. 123.

118. Panikkar points out, for instance, that 'the Indian soldier who fought on the Marne came back to India with other ideas of the Sahib than those he was taught to believe by decades of official propaganda (p. 262). The historian I Spector has characterised the Russian popular rising in 1905 as 'the French Revolution of Asia' (p. 29).

119. Kolko (1970), pp. 116–18.

120. Bunche, p. 1040.

121. Barraclough (1964), p. 148.

122. *The Times*, London, 3 July 1961. Quoted in Dell, p. 143.

123. Our weakness for irrelevant (?) parallels makes it irresistible to quote the following passage from Ruth Hallden's review of the sixteenth part of Tora Dahl's autobiography: 'Tora Dahl has written one of the books of the century about an intellectual woman's attempt to realise herself — in a society designed by men, governed and controlled by men, and in which even highly intellectual women . . . are automatically considered to have very special aptitudes for boiling potatoes and cleaning windows' (Dagens Nyheter, 17 September 1978). There may be rather obvious reasons why the political women's organisations are in the vanguard of the struggle for a more equitable world order.

124. The figures reported by the UN have been queried by, among others, Kuznets (1972), pp. 185–209.

125. Some Latin American countries probably achieved a fairly rapid growth before the First World War and in the inter-war period (Kuznets (1971), p. 30; Furtado, pp. 31–36). Austin Robinson regards it as probable that several of the Commonwealth countries in Africa attained a definite increase in production during the inter-war period (Robinson, pp. 19–22). Olufemi Ekundare believes that the Nigerian economy must have expanded considerably during the period 1900–45 (Ekundare, p. 103). A. G. Hopkins points to a rapid increase of consumption and internal trade in West Africa during the twentieth century (Hopkins, pp. 244–52). Estimates of the national income of Sri Lanka indicate a very rapid growth during the Second World War (Karunatilake, pp. 2–4). For several developing countries there are statistics which show a relatively rapid growth in exports before the Great War (Maddison (1970), p. 198). It is uncertain, however, if this can be taken as evidence that the aggregate output increased as well. Kenwood and Lougheed present several examples of countries that increased exports very rapidly from 1870 to 1913 without any significant repercussions on the rest of the economy (Kenwood & Lougheed, p. 149).

126. Maddison (1970), pp. 28–29.

127. Kuznets (1971), pp. 30–31.

128. Bairoch, chap. 2 and p. 185.

129. This applies to most of the countries in Latin America and also, for instance, to India, Pakistan, the Philippines, Nigeria, Ghana, Sierra Leone and the Ivory Coast.

130. Svedberg (1977) provides a brief resume of the policy of import substitution.
131. Svedberg (1977) gives a critical account of the hypotheses of these researchers.
132. *Pakistan Economic Journal*, June 1958.
133. Maddison (1971), p. 136.
134. Sveriges samarbete med u-landerna. SOU 1977:13, p. 373. Calculated as a share of the GNP of the wealthy countries, aid has diminished virtually uninterruptedly since 1961.
135. Johnson (1967), pp. 18–23.
136. Radetzki, p. 61; Johnson (1967), p. 91 et seq.
137. Schiavo-Campo & Singer, p. 200.
138. Solomon participated as an American expert in virtually all the important negotiations on international currency questions up to 1975–76.
139. The member states of the UN has never taken an explicit political decision on the delimitation of the group known as developing countries. On the other hand, the statistical office of the UN has in its publications divided the countries of the world into three classes. One of these is usually called the group of developing countries and it includes all the countries and non-selfgoverning territories in Africa, Asia, Latin America and Oceania with the exception of Australia, China, Cyprus, Japan, Mongolia, New Zealand, North Korea, South Africa and Turkey. The World Bank also includes Portugal, Spain, Yugoslavia, Greece, Rumania and Turkey in the group of developing countries. A more detailed account of the definition is to be found in 'Sveriges samarbete med u-landerna', SOU 1977: 13, app. 2.
140. Resources and Man, p. 59.
141. Pincus, pp. 360–67; Schultz.
142. Bairoch, p. 43.
143. UNCTAD (1977), table 2.6.
144. Sveriges samarbete med u-landerna, SOU 1977-14, p. 46.
145. The following section draws largely on Anell (1977).
146. Anell (1977), p. 14.
147. Adam in Radice, pp. 99–100.
148. Barnet & Mueller, p. 157.
149. Black, pp. 236–37.
150. Fong & Lim, p. 20.
151. Lall & Streeten, p. 13.
152. Morton & Tulloch, p. 212.
153. Nayyar, pp. 59–79.
154. During the 1970s a number of developing countries have adopted measures to strengthen their control over the economy. Several sectors have been closed to transnational corporations in a number of developing countries. Colombia, India, Indonesia, Mexico, Pakistan and South Korea are among the developing countries that have introduced legislation intended to prevent foreign capital from taking over national enterprises. The supervision of transnational corporations has been tightened up in practically all of the important host countries. Several Swedish enterprises have, for example, been forced to increase purchases from subcontractors in the local market. These efforts on the part of the developing countries are facilitated by the fact that the transnational corporations are growing in number and come from an increasing variety of countries. Particularly the large, expansive developing countries are thereby put in a position to play off different enterprises against each other in order to obtain more advantageous contracts.
155. IBRD (1978), p. 28.

156. UNCTAD (1979), Table 1.12.
157. The figure given for Taiwan's balance of trade in IBRD (1978) is wrong. The correct figures used here have been obtained by enquiry to the World Bank.
158. Hobsbawn (1975), p. 47.
159. In general, however, the utilisation of capacity was lower than during earlier peaks of trade expansion despite a growth rate of 8 per cent in the seven largest OECD countries during the first half of 1973.
160. van Cleveland & Brittain.
161. Beim; Grjebine; Ensor.
162. Solomon, p. 187.
163. Solomon, p. 270.
164. Whitman.

2. THE DEVELOPING COUNTRIES' DEMANDS FOR A NEW INTERNATIONAL ECONOMIC ORDER

THE DEVELOPING COUNTRIES' DEMANDS EVOLVE

Early in the twentieth century the developing countries attempted to organise some mutual cooperation to give added weight to their common demand. Thus a Pan-African Congress assembled in Paris in 1919 to persuade the architects of the Peace of Versailles to declare the right of Africans to participate in colonial administration. Neither this nor the following three congresses in the 1920s achieved their aim, however, and it was a tenuous tradition that Kwame Nkrumah took up again when in 1958, the year after Ghana's independence, he tried to resuscitate the Pan-African movement by convening a conference in Accra.

The Soviet Communist Party made some attempts during the inter-war period to organise the colonial population against the colonial powers. Thus representatives of thirty-seven nationalities were gathered in 1920 for a 'Conference of the Peoples of the East'. Within the Pan-Islamic movement contacts were maintained between Muslims from all over the world — from Indonesia in the east to Morocco in the west.

Yet the starting point for the developing country movement must be said to be the *Asian-African Conference in Bandung*, Indonesia, in 1955. Representatives of twenty-nine independent countries gathered there at the invitation of the prime ministers of Burma, India, Indonesia, Pakistan and Sri Lanka. Among the countries represented were the People's Republic of China and Japan. This took place in the middle of the cold war. The conference was followed with great interest by governments and mass media in the West — a situation that was not to recur until the OPEC countries quadrupled the export price of oil.

Political independence was naturally the central issue at the Bandung conference. Thus the president of the host country,

Sukarno, sharply attacked racism and colonialism. The colonial powers were held to have forfeited their right to administer the remaining colonies as they had not fulfilled the obligations stipulated in the section of the UN Charter that deals with non-selfgoverning territories.

It should be noted, however, that the meeting also adopted a number of principles for economic cooperation which were to become the basis for the demands later advanced at international conferences. They can also be seen as an embryonic form of the Declaration and Programme of Action for the Establishment of a New International Economic Order that were adopted by the UN General Assembly almost 20 years later. Among the proposals in the economic sphere were the stabilisation of the prices and demand for raw materials and increased processing of raw materials in the Third World (1).

Reactions to this manifestation by a group of states that had shown themselves determined to prove their independence of the major powers of both East and West were, in the atmosphere of the Cold War, often very negative.

It was not until 1961, however, that a better defined co-ordinative organisation for developing countries was established. The pace-setters among the third world leaders, men like Nasser, Nehru, Nkrumah, Sukarno and Tito, collaborated in organising a conference in Belgrade, Yugoslavia, at which principles were laid down for the *Non-Aligned Movement*. Membership of the movement was extended to states that did not belong to any bilateral or collective military alliance and did not allow the major powers to occupy military bases on their territory (2).

The movement aimed to work for decolonisation, non-interference in the internal affairs of sovereign states, peaceful co-existence, opposition to great power politics, disarmament, and the strengthening of the United Nations. At the forefront, therefore, stood principles and measures that could contribute to the protection of the right of the new states to exist. On the other hand, less attention was paid within the movement to measures that could contribute to economic development. Economic questions were at that time regarded as technical matters which did not require to be dealt with at a high political level (3). The need for such measures had nevertheless begun to be appreciated internationally and had led in 1961, i.e. the very year in which the movement was launched, to the adoption at the UN of a programme for economic development. At the same time, the 1960s were designated *the First Development Decade*.

The target for the First Development Decade was that every developing country should achieve an annual economic growth of at least 5 per cent. With the object of reaching this target the member states of the UN were urged, among other things, to facilitate the chances for developing countries to sell their products at stable and remunerative prices, to take steps to ensure that a larger share of the profits from the exploitation and marketing of the raw materials of the developing countries that were handled by foreign enterprises should go to the developing countries, and to increase the flow of capital, both public and private, to the developing countries on mutually acceptable terms (4).

In a way the UN decision regarding the First Development Decade denotes a change in the character of the organisation. When it was founded in 1945, the principal aim was to create an agency that could provide the basis for an international security system. However, the UN Charter, that was adopted by 51 states, including 33 developing countries, also includes a section on economic and social cooperation and, apart from the General Assembly, the Secretariat and the International Court, an Economic and Social Council and a Trusteeship Council were also set up.

On the initiative of the Americans a discussion began at the UN in 1949 on the organisation's obligations towards its poor members and on the role that the UN should play as a channel for aid. This led to the establishment of EPTA (Expanded Programme of Technical Assistance). During the 1950s, however, the security questions overshadowed those of development and EPTA's operations stagnated. The expenditure of the organisation amounted during virtually the whole of the 1950s to about US $20 millions a year (5).

The rise in the number of member states, the majority of them developing countries, helped to focus ever-increasing attention on development questions.

Table 18 Members of the United Nations.

	1945	1950	1960	1970	1975	1978	1979
Total	51	60	100	127	144	151	152
of which developing countries (members of the group of 77)	33	40	67	94	109	117	118

The operations of existing UN agencies were reoriented and new agencies were formed at a rapid rate in order to tackle the development problems in different spheres. In the sphere of aid EPTA was supplemented by the UN Special Fund and the resources for technical assistance were rapidly enlarged, from about US $38 millions in 1960 to $125 millions by the middle of the first development decade, i.e. 1965. EPTA and the Special Fund were amalgamated in 1965 to form the UN Development Programme (UNDP). The operations of the World Bank were supplemented in 1959 by a special agency to assist the developing countries with development credits on easy terms (IDA, International Development Association). (See also p. 00 et seq.)

In connection with the UN resolution on the First Development Decade the Secretary General was instructed to consult the members regarding the advisability of holding an international conference on trade problems. These consultations eventually made is possible to hold the earlier mentioned first Conference on Trade and Development (*UNCTAD I*) in Geneva in 1964. At this conference the opposition between 'South' and 'North' was accentuated more clearly than before. In preparation for this conference the developing countries had succeeded in coordinating their positions and acted as a unified bloc during the conference. The cooperation that began between the developing countries represented at the conference — their number was reckoned to be seventy-seven and the group has since then been referred to at international conferences as the Group of 77 — established a pattern for subsequent international conferences.

The unity within the Group of 77 was obviously bought at the cost of certain sacrifices. Critics hold that it was the interests of the least developed countries that had to give way to those of the more developed. The strategy adopted by the Group of 77, which primarily aimed at facilitating the sale of exports from developing countries in the markets of industrialised countries, has also been criticised.

'Through UNCTAD they (the developing countries) insist that far more rich and powerful nations, whose policies they cannot control, should alter their pattern of trading and manufacturing in the interests of the developing world. By so doing they increase their dependence and multiply their risks; they narrow their choices of technology; and they distort their pattern of specialization to an external demand which is beyond their control' (6).

The endeavour to achieve unity within the Group of 77 led to an accentuation of the opposition between the developing countries as a whole and the industrialised countries. This was clearly demonstrated when the conference came to consider the proposals that had been drafted for it. The conference adopted a Final Act which embraces 15 general principles for trade between states, a number of special principles and a series of recommendations in a large number of spheres of interest to the developing countries (7). Several of the industrialised countries voted against some of the general principles (the United States voted against most of them) and thus announced that they regarded the Final Act only as a protocol of the proceedings and thus not binding on them (8). For the developing countries, however, the Final Act was to form the basis for their actions and for the demands that were put forward at subsequent international conferences.

With regard to the positions adopted by individual industrialised countries it may be noted that the United States voted against the principles concerning respect for sovereign states and the right of sovereign states to conduct trade with other countries. The Americans also opposed the standpoint of the conference that development problems are problems for which the industrialised and developing countries have a joint responsibility to seek solutions. More significant, perhaps, is the fact that the principles concerning measures which aimed to make it easier for the developing countries to increase their exports to the industrialised countries and to attempt to maintain mutually acceptable ratios between prices for finished products and raw materials met with great resistance. Eight countries voted against and 19 abstained. Those voting against included Australia, Canada, Great Britain and the United States. The eighth principle, which covered special tariff preferences for the developing countries, received even less support. Eleven voted against and 23 countries abstained. The countries that voted against were Australia, Austria, Canada, Iceland, Lichtenstein, Norway, South Africa, Sweden, Switzerland, the United Kingdom and the United States.

In this connection it may also be noted that the Trade and Development Conference was institutionalised and a secretariat for the conference was established in Geneva. Formally this UN organisation is open to all member states and is concerned with global questions. In practice, however, UNCTAD was from the very beginning regarded as the 'trade union' of the developing countries. It is, for example, accepted practice that the developing countries select the Secretary General of UNCTAD in the same way as the United States selects the head of the World Bank and Western Europe the head of the International Monetary Fund.

Despite the fact that the industrialised countries so clearly registered their opposition to contributing towards the improvements in trading conditions for the developing countries that were demanded in the Final Act, the Group of 77 persisted in a strategy for increased integration of the world economy at subsequent conferences. A certain success was also achieved in 1968 when a second Trade and Development Conference took place in New Delhi, India, (*UNCTAD II*), in so far as the industrialised countries agreed to work for the establishment of a system of special tariff preferences for the developing countries (General System of Preferences, GSP). A proposal for such a system, largely drafted within the UNCTAD secretariat under the direction of the organisation's first Secretary General, Raoul Prebisch, had been opposed by all the industrialised countries at the first conference. But the principles of the system adopted in New Delhi had been elaborated by the wealthy countries in the OECD and were more limited in scope than those discussed at UNCTAD I. Only manufactured goods and semi-manufactures were included in the preference system. Even within these groups of merchandise, however, several products of importance to the developing countries were excluded because of the industrialised countries' desire to protect domestic production. Because of the far-reaching agricultural regulations of the OECD no preferences were granted for agricultural products. Most of these could, however, already be imported duty-free (9).

The *meeting* held by the *Non-Aligned States* in *Lusaka*, Zambia, in 1970 differed from previous meetings. The previous antagonism of the movement to big-power politics, colonialism and racism was now less prominent. Instead economic relations emerged as a principal issue for the member states. For the first time the movement adopted a resolution which included positive statements on the necessity of altering the relationship between industrialised and developing countries, and in this context particular importance was attached to cooperation between the developing countries. The concept of self-reliance, which later gained such prominence in the debate about the developing countries, was introduced in the resolution from this meeting.

This reorientation of the movement's activity resulted from the fact that non-alignment lost force as a unifying catchword for the movement during the 1960s, while at the same time domestic development problems mounted up in many developing countries. The tension between the superpowers was gradually reduced. Many former colonies were given political independence and the need to take action on that issue thus diminished. Rothstein also points out that non-alignment as an idea was essential during the period when the new states gave the highest priority to establishing their national identity, but declined in significance in proportion to the growing severity of the economic problems (10).

At the time of the Lusaka conference it was clear that the First Development Decade had not come up to the movement's expectations (see p. 89). 95

— for many developing countries the economic situation had not improved;

— in so far as economic growth had occurred it had often been restricted to the modern sector of the economies of the developing countries and had thus accentuated the differences between the modern and the traditional sector;
— increased imports of consumer and investment goods from the developed countries had changed the consumer goods pattern and production structure and had led to greater dependence on the developed countries (11).

In the discussion about the chances of breaking out of this process, developments in China, which had until then been relatively isolated from the outside world, attracted great interest. This debate led to proposals for measures aimed at promoting cooperation between developing countries in order to reduce their dependence on the industrialised countries.

The declaration adopted at the Lusaka meeting formed the basis for the line taken by the developing countries in the discussion that was later conducted during the 25th Session of the UN General Assembly in 1970 on *the Second Development Decade*.

Many initiatives had been taken with the aim of creating a basis for discussing the strategy for the Second Development Decade, the 1970s. At the meeting a report was presented which had been drafted under the direction of the Canadian ex-premier Lester B. Pearson, 'Partners in Development'. In this report 67 recommendations were made in regard to various spheres such as trade, private investments in developing countries, aid and the organisation of aid agencies within the UN system. In addition, there were reports from UNCTAD, from a group of experts led by the Dutch economist, Jan Tinbergen, and a report on the ability of the UN system to handle a larger development programme, compiled by a group led by Sir Robert Jackson (12).

In view of the increased gulfs between industrialised and developing countries, more ambitious targets were established at the UN meeting for the Second Development Decade than for the first (13). The target for economic growth was set at 6 per cent, as an average for the developing countries as a whole, while growth per capita should average 3.5 per cent. Growth of that order would demand an increase in agricultural production of 4 per cent a year and in industrial production of 8 per cent a year.

It is also laid down in the resolution that development ultimately aims to improve the chances for all people to have a better life. To achieve this, incomes and wealth should be more evenly distributed. It is furthermore necessary to increase employment and to ensure people of a more dependable income.

The resolution also suggests more concrete measures in such fields as trade, economic cooperation and development finance in order to reach the established targets. One such measure is that the industrialised countries shall facilitate the access of products from the developing countries to the markets of the industrialised countries by lowering the tariffs on such products. In addition, the industrialised countries should increase their aid to at least 0.7 per cent of their GNP by the middle of the development decade.

It is worth noting that the discussion conducted in Lusaka about measures to strengthen cooperation between the developing countries is not reflected in the resolution from the General Assembly.

At the *meeting of foreign ministers of the Non-Aligned Movement in Georgetown, Guyana, in 1972* the ideas on cooperation between the developing countries were elaborated further (14). A programme of action for economic cooperation was adopted which provides for measures in the following main spheres:

— self-reliance;
— cooperation in trade, transport and industrial development;
— private foreign investments;
— cooperation in research, science and technology including the transfer of technology and technical know-how.

In addition, the programme laid down that four member states should be allocated responsibility for ensuring that measures provided for in the programme were followed up and carried through.

During the discussion about the programme for economic cooperation the question also arose of a permanent secretariat for the movement. This question had been dealt with at previous conferences but had not gained sufficient support. At first, many member states appear to have feared that a firmer organisation of the movement would be regarded as a provocation by the major powers. But later it seems that disagreement on questions such as the allocation of tasks to, and location of, the proposed secretariat were the main obstacles to its creation. In Georgetown the proposal to establish a secretariat also fell through and as a compromise a proposal was adopted to hold more frequent ministerial meetings to supervise the execution of the cooperation programme (15).

The meetings of heads of state of the Non-Aligned Movement in Algiers in 1973 brought together more delegates than ever before. At the meeting in Belgrade in 1961 there were 25 participating states. By 1970 the membership had increased to 53 and at the conference in Algiers, 75 states were represented. The economic questions were now given an even more prominent place than before and at the meeting a declaration and an action programme for economic cooperation were adopted (16). Compared to resolutions from previous meetings, this represented an essential widening of the outlook of the movement on economic development. Much of the content of the programme derived from the positions adopted by the Group of 77 in these matters.

The declaration of the meeting did, however, refer back to earlier declarations which had been directed more to considerations of security policy. It points out, for example, that not only war but also poverty and deteriorating economic conditions are antitheses of peace.

The viewpoints that were advanced in the declaration and the programme not only involved an extension of the sphere within which the movement would express opinions, but also represented a sharpening of its formulations on many points. This applied, for instance, on the question of the right to dispose over natural resources. At the conference in Belgrade in 1961 the principle that member states should have the right of full command over their natural resources had been laid down, but with the important rider that this right should be enjoyed without breaking agreements already entered into and should be based on the principle of mutual benefit and international right.

At the Algiers conference a principle of unconditional right to command natural resources was instead laid down and nationalisation of those under foreign ownership was seen as a legitimate means of protecting one's resources. Any conflicts that might arise in connection with nationalisation were to be settled in accordance with national legislation in each state. Later, at the Sixth Special Session of the UN, President Boumedienne even said that 'nationalisation is a stage of development' (17).

Trade and monetary matters were also dealt with in depth at the Algiers meeting. Against the background of what was seen as a structural imbalance in world trade, characterised by a diminishing share for the developing countries and a progressive deterioration of the terms of trade for the products of developing countries, it was suggested that the general system of preferences for developing countries (GSP) should be extended. Discrimination in favour of the developing countries without a corresponding obligation on the latter to give preferential treatment to exports from industrialised countries should be written into the rules of GATT (18) (see p. 59 et seq.). The trade questions were particularly relevant at the time of the Algiers meeting, as a new round of comprehensive multilateral trade negotiations within the framework of GATT were to begin in Tokyo only a week or so afterwards (19).

Criticism of the monetary system became considerably sharper. Previously the system had been accepted as such, even if certain changes had been suggested. Now the system was regarded as having satisfied only the interests of the industrialised countries and for that reason a new system was demanded that would guarantee the participation of the developing countries on the same terms as the industrialised countries, as well as stability in financial flows. It was proposed that a link should be established between SDRs (see p. 50) and additional development financing and that the industrialised countries should accept a plan with a time limit for the fulfilment of the aid targets that had been written into the strategy for the Second Development Decade (see p. 94).

With regard to private foreign investments the need to work out a common standpoint had already been discussed at earlier meetings. At the Algiers meeting the operational methods of the transnational corporations were rejected as unacceptable. The meeting recommended joint actions aimed, inter alia, at adopting common rules for transnational corporations, to support nationalisation measures and to establish a centre for the gathering of information on the operations of transnational enterprises.*

When proposals were considered by the meeting with regard to the transfer of technology, further criticism was directed against monopolistic principles of the transnational corporations. Demands were made for the adoption of new international legislation in the form of a code of conduct regarding the transfer of technology. In addition, urgent action was called for to stop the emigration of qualified manpower from the developing countries.

Environmental questions had been given some attention in Georgetown in 1972. At the Algiers conference it was stated that such questions are, on the whole, only of interest to industrialised countries.

In the discussion on transport, states expressed their support of the code of conduct for liner conferences that had been drafted within UNCTAD (see p. 143 et seq.).

Finally the declaration contained a statement of strong support for economic cooperation between the member countries, above all in the spheres of trade, transport and industrial development. Measures were suggested for facilitating the establishment and further development of producer cooperation and of promoting joint marketing ventures.

The conference also decided to address a request to the Secretary General of the UN that a Special Session of the UN General Assembly should be convened to discuss development problems. This matter was raised during the ordinary Session of the UN later in the autumn and the proposal was approved. The course of events soon after the Algiers meeting was, however, to have the result that the Special Session proposed by the members of the Non-Aligned Movement was preceded by a Special Session on raw materials and development, which

---

* At the Conference of Foreign Ministers in Lima 1975 it was decided to locate such an information centre in Havana.

turned out to be the one at which the debate on development was presented with a new concept — a New International Economic Order. Before we describe that session we shall briefly outline the economic and political events during the autumn and winter of 1973/74.

THE ECONOMICO–POLITICAL PRELUDE TO A NEW INTERNATIONAL ECONOMIC ORDER

During the postwar period the demand for oil has increased very rapidly but, as a result of extensive prospecting, many new fields have been opened up, thus rapidly increasing the supply. Up to the mid-1960s, however, the big corporations — 'the Seven Sisters' — succeeded in controlling production and thereby the price level (20). Subsequently several producers that were independent of the big corporations entered the market and, as a result, the price of crude oil fell in real terms (21). This resulted in smaller profits for the oil corporations and low revenues for the oil-producing states.

The oil states became increasingly dissatisfied with the situation and, at the meetings held by the coordinating organisation OPEC, louder and louder demands for changes were made. Libya took the lead in making demands on the foreign enterprises that were exploiting its oil. In 1970 the Libyan government requested that production should be cut back and that export prices should be raised. This caused a chain reaction in which the 'politically speaking . . . more conservative regimes in the Middle East could not afford to take a more compliant attitude towards the corporations than the "radical" regimes in North Africa' (22).

At an OPEC conference in Caracas in December 1970 the tough attitude of the member countries towards the corporations became even tougher. Decisions were taken to tax profits by at least 55 per cent, to raise export prices in general and establish new bases of calculation for differentiation in respect of the quality of oil and its proximity to the market, and to cancel all discounts on the official export prices.

The oil corporations, which until then had operated under

comparatively heavy competition in part forced on them by the anti-trust legislation of the United States, considered that the situation demanded joint action and were given the go-ahead by the then president of the United States. Some maintain that the American government was in favour of rises in the price of oil, as this might both make the Arab countries more inclined to accept a compromise solution of the Middle East conflict and change the competitive relations between the United States, on the one hand, and Western Europe and Japan on the other (23). The USA had largely relied on its domestic oil reserves and had strictly limited its imports. The domestically produced oil was, however, more expensive than that which could be imported, for instance, from the Middle East. The European countries and Japan had instead exploited the possibilities of importing cheap oil. This had led, in those countries, to a rapid replacement of other energy sources in favour of oil and, in time, to a very large dependence on oil. In 1970 oil provided about 60 per cent of the energy produced in the OECD countries in Europe. The corresponding figure for Japan was at that time over 70 per cent (24).

In 1971 the demands of the OPEC countries were extended to cover partnership in the foreign enterprises. The demand was at first for 20 per cent, but was then changed to a majority shareholding of 51 per cent. In many countries a number of installations were soon nationalised. Thus the Algerian government in February 1971 nationalised 51 per cent of the French concessions. Libya nationalised BP's installations and two years later attained a 51 per cent interest in the other concessions. Before these nationalisation measures only 0.23 per cent of the aggregate production of the OPEC countries was nationally owned (in 1970). By 1975 the share had risen to 61 per cent. The national shareholdings were at that time highest in Iran (96 per cent) and Iraq (85 per cent) (25).

The demands put forward in 1970 for higher prices proved inadequate to compensate for price rises on other goods. In addition, after the rise, the corporations had managed more than adequately to compensate themselves for the increased crude oil prices and had thus succeeded in raising their profits. This led to demands on the part of the OPEC states for additional rises.

The action which was thus being prepared by the OPEC states was facilitated by the pronounced economic upswing that occurred in almost all the OECD countries during the first years of the 1970s.

The economic upswing caused an increase in demand not only for oil but also for many other raw materials, which therefore rose in price. Wage claims also intensified. The increased prices of raw materials and labour boosted prices for manufactured goods. The consequent rate of inflation was one of the highest recorded since the early 1950s. The price increases also extended to agricultural products, especially grain, for which the heavier demand from many developing countries, as well as from the Soviet Union, due to drought and harvest failures, made prices shoot up. The price trend for raw materials and finished products is shown in the table below.

Table 19   Export prices of agricultural products, minerals and manufactures (Index 1963 = 100).

	1963	1970	1972	1973	1974	1975	1976	1977
Agricultural products	100	107	125	185	235	225	230	255
Minerals (including fuels and non-ferrous metals)	100	122	147	195	440	450	510	550
Manufactures	100	114	131	152	185	212	212	232

Source: GATT International Trade 1977/78, p. 2.

At the beginning of the 1970s, a debate began about the finiteness of raw materials which had been initiated by the report 'The Limits of Growth' commissioned by the Club of Rome. Some believe that the lively debate on the scarcity of world resources helped prepare public opinion for the subsequent oil-price rises and to make them appear legitimate in the eyes of the general public (26).

Among other factors which may have contributed to the subsequent rises of oil prices were the increased demand caused by the economic upswing in 1972, the shortage of refining capacity and a temporary shortage of tanker tonnage.

At OPEC's conference in Vienna in October 1973 demands

were made for substantial rises in crude oil prices. Negotiations were started with representatives of the oil corporations, but after consultations with the governments of their respective 'home countries' they announced that they could not agree to the rises proposed by OPEC. The price increase was then fixed at about 70 per cent, i.e. an increase from US $3.00 to US $ 5.11 a barrel. A few months later, at a meeting in Teheran, the OPEC countries decided once again to raise the price of oil, this time from US $5.11 to US $11.65 with effect from 1 January 1974. The price then remained at that level throughout 1974. A subsequent decision led to a raising of the price from the beginning of 1976 to US $12.38 (27).

The first large price rise occurred soon after the outbreak of the October war between Egypt and Israel. The situation became more acute when the Arab countries also decided to cut off the oil supply to countries that were regarded as being favourably inclined towards Israel, such as the USA and the Netherlands. The boycott and price rises clearly showed what power the oil states possessed when they could act in unison against the oil corporations and industrialised countries.

Not unexpectedly, the actions of the OPEC countries resulted in counter-measures by the consumer countries. In January 1974 the US government invited the major consumer countries to a conference in Washington to work out a common strategy to solve the energy crisis. Certain consumer countries feared that such a conference would lead to an unnecessary confrontation, especially with the Arab countries. Thus the President of France put forward a proposal that an international conference should be held on energy questions, if possible within the framework of the UN. This initiative did not, however, succeed in preventing the Washington conference from being held. At the latter no joint statement on the price question was delivered, but on the part of the United States it was made clear that a change in the price level would be sought in order to establish an equitable price — lower than the current one but higher than that applying in September 1973. (The decisions at the conference subsequently led to an agreement on an international energy programme that was to be put into effect by an International Energy Agency — the Oil Club — which was established within the framework of the OECD in 1974.)

In that situation Algeria's President Boumedienne, in his capacity as chairman of the Non-Aligned Movement, directed a request to the Secretary General of the UN that a Special Session of the General Assembly should be convened to study raw materials and development problems. As this initiative immediately received widespread support, such a conference could soon take place.

UN DECISION ON A NEW INTERNATIONAL ECONOMIC ORDER

The Sixth Special Session of the General Assembly of the United Nations in April 1974 was to be historical at least in one respect. It was the first time that a session of the General Assembly was entirely devoted to development problems. On this occasion decisions were taken, albeit of a non-binding nature, which express the need for a new order to achieve a more than even distribution of resources, to reduce the gap between developing and industrialised countries, to guarantee economic and social progress in the developing countries, and to secure peace and justice for the present and future generations.

A long list of demands from the developing countries, some of which had previously been rejected by the industrialised countries, were now incorporated in a Declaration and Programme of Action for the Establishment of a New International Economic Order, and resolutions on three documents were adopted without being put to the vote (28).

In order to explain this apparently remarkable turn of events it is important to keep in mind that the successful OPEC manoeuvre had raised hopes in many developing countries that similar tactics could be used to force the industrialised countries to make concessions. At the same time there was great uncertainty in the industrialised countries about the real significance and consequences of the oil price rises. Estimates of the financial resources that would accrue to the oil states varied widely, and presumably few governments of industrialised countries were fully aware that an unusually deep and prolonged economic recession had begun.

The preparatory work for the conference appears to have been handled by the members of the Group of 77, while the group of industrialised countries remained fairly passive. The basis for the discussions by the developing countries was the documents that had been adopted at the meeting of the non-aligned states in Algiers, and the Final Act adopted by the General Assembly after five weeks of negotiation bears a large resemblance to the Algiers documents.

The division into two main documents, a declaration and a programme of action, was the same. While the Algiers declaration contains an account and discussion of economic conditions in developing countries, the UN declaration starts with an assertion of the need to establish a new international economic order, which is followed by the enumeration of 20 principles on which the new order shall rest (29). Among the most fundamental of these principles are the following (30):

— Sovereign equality of States, self-determination of all peoples, inadmissibility of the acquisition of territories by force, territorial integrity and non-interference in the internal affairs of other States;
— The broadest co-operation of all the States members of the international community, based on equity, whereby the prevailing disparities in the world may be banished and prosperity secured for all;
— The right of every country to adopt the economic and social system that it deems the most appropriate for its own development and not to be subjected to discrimination of any kind as a result;
— Full permanent sovereignty of every State over its natural resources and all economic activities;
— Regulation and supervision of the activities of transnational corporations by taking measures in the interest of the national economies of the countries where such transnational corporations operate on the basis of the full sovereignty of those countries;
— Just and equitable relationship between the prices of raw materials, primary commodities, manufactured and semi-

manufactured goods exported by developing countries and the prices of raw materials, primary commodities, manufactures, capital goods and equipment imported by them with the aim of bringing about sustained improvement in their unsatisfactory terms of trade and the expansion of the world economy;
— Ensuring that one of the main aims of the reformed international monetary system shall be the promotion of the development of the developing countries and the adequate flow of real resources to them;
— Preferential and non-reciprocal treatment for developing countries, wherever feasible, in all fields of international economic co-operation whenever possible;
— Facilitating the role which producers' associations may play within the framework of international co-operation.

The action programme also suggests how certain of the principles are to be realised. The programme is divided into 10 sections which deal with fundamental problems concerning the significance of raw materials for trade and development, the international monetary system and the financing of the progress of the developing countries, industrialisation, the transfer of technology, and the regulation and control of the operations of the transnational enterprises.

Compared to the action programme adopted at the Algiers conference the UN programme is somewhat more elaborate. Thus the section dealing with raw material questions — which in the Algiers document is chiefly devoted to sovereignty over natural resources, exploitation of natural resources to promote self-reliance, and the relative decline in prices for raw materials and producer cooperation — has been expanded to include a proposal for a link between the prices of the developing countries' exports and imported goods. Proposals have also been added to the section on trade for an integrated commodity programme and repayment to the developing countries of the tariffs which the industrialised countries levy on their products (31). A separate section of the UN programme also deals with emergency measures to mitigate the difficulties of the developing countries which have been most severely affected by the 'economic crisis'.

The discussions during the Sixth Special Session dealt primarily with the section on permanent sovereignty over natural resources, the demand for an equitable relationship between the prices for the products exported by the developing countries and those imported by them, as well as the establishment of producer associations between developing countries for the most important raw materials (32). These questions were also taken up in many of the 39 declarations of intent and reservations submitted after the decision on the declaration and programme of action. Concerning the demand for sovereignty over natural resources many industrialised countries did in fact accept the right to nationalisation, but asserted that compensation should be paid in accordance with international law. This was regarded as unacceptable by the developing countries in view of the fact that current international law has been created by and for the benefit of the industrialised countries.

Although there were many questions on which the delegates of the developing countries had very divergent opinions and interests, they succeeded in maintaining a united front against the industrialised country bloc. It may be appropriate here to point out that the Soviet Union and other East European countries have traditionally adopted a passive attitude to debates at the UN on the developing countries. They have said, though this may be somewhat oversimplifying their views, that the problems of the developing countries are the result of colonialism and that it is therefore the task of the former colonial powers to solve the problems. In the Soviet Union's contribution to the debate the emphasis was laid on the significance of security policies for international development. Support was expressed for fundamental principles in the declaration on national sovereignty over natural resources and economic activity. The Chinese contribution showed that China fully identified itself with the developing countries. The Chinese delegate pointed out that 'all developing countries were in varying degrees subjected to superpower control, threats or harassment' (33). On those grounds the principles of self-reliance in the declaration were supported by China.

As a result of the procedure for adopting the declaration and programme of action (by so-called consensus decision) the meeting arrived at a decision on far-reaching changes in the world economy which gave the impression of reflecting the views of an unanimous assembly. No state had openly opposed the decision by demanding a vote. There is nothing, however, to indicate that the differences of opinion had been bridged at the meeting. The uncertainty of the industrialised countries as to the significance of the altered negotiation position merely led them to change the external forms of their stand — from openly declared views to reservations in the form of declarations of intent.

FROM DECISIONS TO PRACTICAL ACTION

The Sixth Special Session of the General Assembly was followed shortly by a long series of international conferences at which parts of the adoption declaration and programme of action were taken up for further discussion.

In August 1974 a *World Population Conference* was held in *Bucharest*. The proceedings of the Conference were marked by the political atmosphere that had ensued from the Sixth Special Session of the General Assembly. 'The stress laid on economic power relations in the world which thereby came to colour not least the plan of action of the conference may at the same time be seen as expressing the desire of many developing countries to emphasise that population growth does not constitute the principal cause of the poverty of the developing countries' (34).

At the 1974 Ordinary Session of the UN General Assembly, a Charter of Economic Rights and Duties of States was adopted (33). A demand for such a charter had arisen at the third UNCTAD conference in Santiago, Chile, in 1972. The charter incorporates principles that should provide guidance for economic, political and other relations between states, the rights and duties of states and the responsibilities of countries towards the international community.

Many of the principles included in the declaration from the Sixth Special Session reappear in the charter in the form of an international agreement. On certain matters the charter goes beyond the declaration. This applies, for example to the question of compensation in the case of nationalisation — the rules stipulating that compensation is to be paid in accordance with national law. Most of the industrialised countries were not prepared to accept that and 16 of them voted against this paragraph.

In the autumn of 1974 a declaration was adopted at the *World Food Conference in Rome* about eradicating hunger and malnutrition, as well as resolutions covering such measures as to increase food production, improve the level of nutrition, increase and liberalise trade and secure the world's supply of foodstuffs. The resolutions also included a decision to set up a special fund to finance agricultural development (36).

The positions of the *non-aligned states* were elaborated further at a *ministerial conference in Dakar*, Senegal, in February 1975. The document adopted at that meeting is regarded as being the ideologically most thoroughly prepared one adopted by the movement. It is to a large extent based on the so-called centre-periphery theories elaborated by Raul Prebish, Samir Amin, Andre Gundar Frank and others, and also reflects the increased influence of Marxist trains of thought within the movement.

'In brief, the Non-aligned countries argued that the development of the rich capitalist countries is intimately related to the colonial and neo-colonial exploitation of the periphery' . . . 'The Third World functions as a reservoir of raw materials and cheap labor power, contributing to the development of the center while indigenous social systems are disrupted and third world societies are less able to satisfy their own basic needs than they were before the colonial period. Any "development" that occurs is distorted and uneven, involving only a small part of the population and confining itself to sectoral and regional enclaves' (37).

Raw material questions stood in the forefront before the conference. In a programme of action adopted by the conference it is suggested that the member states should establish buffer stocks and undertake market interventions or other actions with the aim of stabilising prices for the exporting countries and of guaranteeing supplies to the importing countries. Such operations should be organised by the producer countries and the idea was that financing would be arranged through a solidarity fund established with contributions from various developing countries, primarily the OPEC countries. In addition, the conference discussed industrial questions, which were shortly afterwards also to be dealt with at the *Second General Conference of UNIDO* held in *Lima, Peru*. The latter also adopted a Declaration and Programme of Action for Industrial Development and Cooperation which established as one of its aims that the developing countries' share of industrial production should increase to the maximum possible extent and preferably reach at least 25 per cent by the year 2000. The only country that voted against the documents was the United States (38).

In February 1975 a Trade and Aid Agreement (the *Lome Convention*) was concluded between the EEC states and 46 states in Africa, the Caribbean and the Pacific region (ACP). This agreement supersedes the agreements which the EEC previously had with certain states in Africa, but in comparison with earlier agreements it represents considerably improved conditions for the ACP states. Among other things, the ACP states are guaranteed trade in industrial products on non-reciprocal conditions (free access to the EEC markets without the states having to guarantee the EEC any particular advantages in return), together with stabilisation of the revenues from certain raw materials and increased aid (39).

In September 1975 the *UN General Assembly* held its *Seventh Special Session* on development and international economic cooperation (40). During this session the negotiating atmosphere was quite different from what it was during the sixth. The uncertainty felt by the industrialised countries in assessing the increased economic and political power of the developing countries had now diminished. The shift of power had not been as great as many had feared. This obviously influenced the industrial countries' will to negotiate and the long drawn out negotiations were not particularly fruitful. Several of the recommendations from the Sixth Special Session were toned down. The more concrete proposals were remitted for further study and negotiations. These were to take place at the planned

UNCTAD conference in Nairobi, Kenya, in the summer of 1976 and in the so-called North–South dialogue in Paris.

At the *meeting of the Group of 77 in Manila in 1976* the developing countries gave their backing to a proposal elaborated by UNCTAD for a so-called integrated commodity programme aimed at improving the terms of trade of the developing countries, reducing the fluctuations in commodity prices and stabilising export revenues. This proposal became one of the main points at the UNCTAD conference (*UNCTAD IV*). Other important points for discussion were the question of the developing countries' burden of debt and the transfer of technology. The industrialised countries were very disunited about the commodity programme. The conference did succeed, however, in uniting on a declaration of principle on the desirability of establishing price-regulating buffer stocks for ten important commodities with the aim of stabilising the export revenues of the developing countries, and that negotiations on the commodity programme should continue (41).

Soon after the UNCTAD conference, the *fifth meeting of heads of state of the Non-Aligned Movement* took place in *Colombo, Sri Lanka*. The setbacks in Nairobi led to sharp reactions in Colombo. Disagreements between the more radical members of the movement, who advocated a harder attitude towards the industrialised countries, and the more moderate ones were also clearly observable. Thus in a comment on a resolution elaborated by the Cuban delegation the Singapore chief delegate said: 'The question I asked myself as I read through the draft resolutions submitted to this conference was: Who am I uniting with and for what objectives and purposes and against whom?' . . . 'These countries are being militant about changing a system upon which they do not depend' (42).

Disagreement within the movement concerning relations with the industrialised countries was, however, covered up as far as possible and instead the emphasis in the resolution was laid on measures to promote cooperation between the developing countries. Among other things a proposal was adopted concerning the establishment of an international bank for developing countries with the aim of reducing their dependence on international reserve currencies and of setting up an agency to advise producer associations.

The North–South Dialogue (Conference on International Economic Cooperation, CIEC), which was begun in Paris in 1975, was brought about by an initiative taken by the President of France with the object of arranging discussions between industrialised and developing countries on energy problems. The developing countries opposed negotiations dealing only with energy questions, however, and the dialogue was widened to cover raw materials, development and financing. The conference was conducted between representatives of 27 states, 19 developing countries and 8 industrialised countries (43).

When the dialogue was concluded in June 1977, it was apparent that few concrete results had been achieved. Some disappointment about this was expressed in the Final Act. And once again a conference had to be concluded amid hopes that better results might be achieved in continued negotiations in other fora.

Those who had been enthusiastic about the developing countries forcing through a decision at the UN for a new international economic order were very disappointed at the subsequent course of events. They reacted in particular against the negotiations being removed from the UN, which was dominated by the developing countries, to a forum created by the industrialised countries on their own terms. After the conclusion of the North–South dialogue, however, the NIEO negotiations were brought back to the UN system.

On the initiative of the whole group of developing countries a *Committee of the Whole* of the General Assembly was then formed with the aim of hastening the negotiations for a New International Economic Order within various UN agencies. The committee held its first session in February 1978. It turned out, however, that the industrialised and developing countries held different views on the mandate of the committee. It was therefore unable to commence its work pending clarification from the General Assembly. (This was given at the end of October 1978.)

In September 1978 a *UN Conference on Technical Cooperation* between *Developing Countries* (TCDC) was held in Buenos Aires, Argentina. Industrialised and developing countries managed, albeit with some difficulty, to agree there on a plan of action. This involves, inter alia, proposals to establish an institution to promote bilateral cooperation between developing countries. In addition, the industrialised countries are urged to revise the rules for their aid, so that it can more easily be used to finance cooperation between developing countries.

Cooperation among developing countries was also one of the items on the agenda before UNCTAD V which was held in Manila, the Philippines in May–June 1979. A programme for cooperation was formulated and the Secretariat was requested to continue work in this field.

However, on the whole, UNCTAD V failed to achieve much. A wide range of issues were on the agenda but few resolutions were made and many of the most important matters had to be referred to the permanent machinery of UNCTAD. Among those was the whole question of the development of world trade, as well as monetary matters and guidelines for debt rescheduling.

The Conference did succeed in formulating a programme for assistance to the least developed countries and to recommend the UN General Assembly to convene a special conference on the problems of the least developed countries. It was also decided that negotiations on the code of conduct for transfer of technology should be resumed. Furthermore, the donor countries were urged to increase their aid.

In August 1979 another major UN Conference was held. That was the UN Conference on Science and Technology which took place in Vienna, Austria. At this conference, the developing countries managed somewhat better in getting response to their demands. As proposed by them, the Conference decided to reorganise the activities of the UN in the field of science and technology and to establish a special fund in order to strengthen the scientific and technological capacity of the developing countries.

Still, more than five years after the UN decisions on the New International Economic Order, many of the components of the Action Programme are far from being implemented. Looking back on what the developing countries have achieved so far, one can record that a large number of negotiations have been set in motion in many spheres. It is hardly an exaggeration, however, to assert that few concrete results have been achieved through these negotiations. It may be too early to expect any. International negotiations can be very complicated and time-consuming. Many proposals also require careful preparatory work, such as those on price stabilisation and codes of conduct for transnational corporations and the transfer of technology. The main explanation, however, must be sought in the changed negotiation strength of the two sides.

The initiative taken by the developing countries in convening the Sixth Special Session of the UN General Assembly gave them for a short period an advantage over the industrialised countries, but this advantage they were unable to sustain. One reason for this is that exceptional circumstances had given the developing countries the chance to put forward their demands at the Sixth Special Session and to have them taken seriously. The further advance of the position of the developing countries necessary for the progress of subsequent negotiations never took place due to internal contention within the bloc of developing countries. In addition, the industrialised countries soon discovered that the threat from the developing countries to restrict the supply of raw materials and oil was less of a problem in economic recession than those of maintaining demand, of defence against competition from the newly industrialising countries and of finding new markets for their products (44).

That the Non-Aligned Movement did not appreciably succeed after the Algiers meeting in further developing its programme may be explained by the fact that the differences of opinion on economic development strategy — development towards increased self-reliance or increased integration in the world economy — are displayed more clearly than before, and thereby the differences in political sympathies with various big power blocs have also emerged. For a long time the movement attracted states that, despite pronounced sympathies with one or other of the superpowers, preferred to adopt a neutral position. As the tension between the superpowers has now been reduced, those states are beginning to advocate a closer association with the superpower to which they are sympathetic. This applies above all to countries like Cuba and Laos, on the one hand, and certain Arab and Latin American countries on the other (45). The rivalry between these various groups was clearly displayed at the foreign ministers' meeting in Belgrade in August 1978, during the discussion on the agenda for the Sixth Summit of Non-Aligned Countries which was held in Havana, Cuba in September 1979. Political controversies within the movement were demonstrated more clearly during that summit than ever before. However, despite these controversies, the conference manages to take some concrete steps forward.

A resolution was adopted which provides policy guidelines on reinforcement of collective self-reliance among Non-Aligned countries and other Third World countries. Also, the conference endorsed an Algerian proposal for a global round of negotiations within the UN embracing energy, trade, money and finance technology as well as development. This proposal is to be launched at the Special Session of the UN General Assembly on development which is to be held during 1980 (46).

Apart from the divergencies of the developing countries, the lack of a permanent secretariat has also hampered the ability of the developing countries to pursue 'their' questions. As before, the preparatory work for international negotiations is done mainly by the UN agencies and by organisations based in the industrialised countries. Nor have independent groups in the developing countries, such as the Third World Forum or Third World Economists, been able to gather sufficient resources to pursue any particularly significant research and fact-finding work. However, many in the third world camp think the time is ripe to reassess and revise the positions adopted by those countries and to seek to strengthen the organisational structure (47). In the light of the increased differences both as regards economic development and political orientation, however, such a revision and consolidation seems to be no easy matter. Nevertheless, decisions were taken at the meeting of the Group of 77 in Arusha in March to appoint an expert group headed by S. S. Ramphal, Secretary General of the Commonwealth Secretariat to formulate proposal for the establishment of a Third World Secretariat. The Third World Forum is also working actively to formulate a proposal to that effect.

Among the organisations or networks based in the industrialised countries which have been involved in or have themselves taken the initiative to facilitate and hasten the NIEO negotiations are the RIO Foundation, International Foundation for Development Alternatives, Society for International Development and the Brandt Commission (Independent Commission on International Development Issues). These have mainly sought to contribute to the Special Session of the UN General Assembly which is planned to take place in 1980.

The feeble economic growth in the industrialised countries has undoubtedly had a negative effect on their willingness to negotiate. There now seems to be little likelihood of the principles of the new order being put into practice in the near future in order to give the developing countries a greater share of the world's resources.

The realisation that the developing countries have contributed during the economic recession to maintaining employment in the industrialised countries by increasing their demand for the products of the latter may, however, influence the negotiation climate. The new catch-word in the development debate, interdependence, reflects a fundamental change of reality. The economic well being of the industrialised countries is increasingly dependent on the developing countries and that may change the basis for future negotiations.

Notes

1. UNITAR, pp. 2–5.
2. ibid., pp. 6–10.
3. Jankowitsch & Sauvant, p. 17.
4. UNITAR, pp. 831–32.
5. Heppling, pp. 9–20, 186.
6. Hunter quoted in Rothstein (1977), p. 148.
7. UNITAR, pp. 35–90.
8. The first three of the general principles are:
   (1) Economic relations between countries, including trade relations, shall be based on respect for the principle of sovereign equality of States, self-determination of peoples, and non-interference in the internal affairs of other countries. 113 for, 1 against (United States) and 2 abstentions (Portugal and Great Britain).

(2) There shall be no discrimination on the basis of differences in socio-economic system. Adaptation of trading methods shall be consistent with this principle. 96 for, 3 against (United States, Canada and West Germany) and 16 abstentions.

(3) Every country has the sovereign right freely to trade with other countries and freely to dispose over its natural resources in the interest of economic development and the well-being of its own people. 94 for, 4 against (Australia, United States, Canada and Great Britain) and 18 abstentions.

9. Rothstein (1977), p. 150.
10. Rothstein (1977), pp. 125–127.
11. Jankowitsch & Sauvant, pp. 17–18.
12. King.
13. Resolution 2626 (XXV) International Development Strategy for the United Nations' Second Development Decade. UNITAR, pp. 856–865.
14. Jankowitsch & Sauvant, p. 21.
    UNITAR, pp. 378–390.
15, The current affairs are now handled by a coordination committee made up of the UN ambassadors of the member states, which meets in New York. See Jankowitsch & Sauvant, p. 14 and Mendis, p. 42.
16. UNITAR, pp. 408–443.
17. Jankowitsch & Sauvant (1976), pp. 32–36.
18. UNITAR, pp. 412–449.
19. ibid., pp. 444–449.
20. Willrich, pp. 29–30.
21. Bjork, p. 29.
22. ibid., p. 45 et seq.
23. Odell, pp. 192–196. According to an article in *Business Week* (July 24, 1978) the oil price rises have, among other things, enabled the United States to strengthen its economic position *vis-a-vis* Europe and Japan.
24. Bjork, p. 38.
25. ibid., pp. 48–51.
26. Odell, p. 196.
27. Blair, pp. 262–262. The price of oil has then risen further. In June 1979 OPEC decided on a base price of US $ 23.50 a barrel. (*Financial Times*, June 30 1979.)
28. The complete text is reproduced in Appendix 1.
29. Jankowitsch & Sauvant, p. 41 et seq.
30. See Appendix 1, p. 187 et seq.
31. Jankowitsch & Sauvant, p. 42 et seq.
32. Aktstycken utgivna av UD, Ny serie I:A:24, p. 10 et seq.
33. ibid., pp. 18–19.
34. Aktstycken utgivna av UD, Ny Serie II:27, p. 6.
35. Aktstycken utgivna av UD, Ny Serie A:A:25, p. 192 et seq.
36. Aktstycken utgivna av UD, Ny Serie II:28, p. 35 et seq.
37. Letelier & Moffitt, p. 34 et seq. and UNITAR, pp. 533–537.
38. UNITAR, pp. 631–650.
39. Survey of International Development (March–April 1975). A new Convention effective from 1 March 1980 was concluded in October 1979. The conditions of Lome II represent very limited improvements to those of Lome I.
40. Aktstycken utgivna av UD, Ny Serie 1:A:26.
41. Menon, pp. 19–29. After two years of negotiations, in March 1979, an agreement to the fundamental elements of the Common Fund, which is the basis

for the programme, was reached.

42. *Financial Times*, 19 August 1976.
43. Menon, pp. 30-33. Participants at the conference were Algeria, Argentina, Brazil, Cameroon, Egypt, India, Indonesia, Iran, Iraq, Jamaica, Mexico, Nigeria, Pakistan, Peru, Saudi-Arabia, Venezuela, Yugoslavia, Zaire and Zambia as representatives of the developing countries and for the industrialised countries Australia, Canada, Japan, Spain, the United States, Sweden and Switzerland together with the European Economic Community.
44. Barraclough (1978a), pp. 45-53 and (1978b), pp. 47-58.
45. Mates, pp. 291-301; Rithstein (1976), pp. 598-616.
46. Raghaven, pp. 99-103.
47. Haq, pp. 181-183.

PART II

4. MOVING TOWARDS A NEW INTERNATIONAL ECONOMIC ORDER

The title we have given to this chapter will probably strike many as unduly optimistic. It is therefore necessary for us to define our terms. The world economy is probably moving towards a new order, but it is very uncertain what form it may take. It seems likely that initially — maybe for quite a long time — we shall experience a growing disorder: a world order that muddles along with the aid of temporary emergency solutions. And perhaps it is only a pious hope that the problems thereby created will eventually increase demand for a working order in which the common interest of all states in participating will act as a cohesive force.

Before we set about considering these problems, however, we shall attempt to answer a number of questions which at first sight may seem trivial.

WHAT ACTUALLY IS AN INTERNATIONAL ECONOMIC ORDER?

An international economic order must reasonably refer broadly to the rules of the game which regulate the economic cooperation of sovereign states in various spheres and which are sustained by the existing distribution of power. These rules include the charters and procedures for decision-making of international organisations as well as other rules, regulations and norms. The system applies to states but also to other actors in the international arena, e.g. transnational corporations, shipping companies and individual human beings. This definition is not very precise but it will have to suffice for the time being.

119

A few points must be noted, however. The international economic order consists of a number of sub-orders. We could for example, in line with Robert Solomon, define the 'international monetary system as the set of arrangements, rules, practices, and institutions under which payments are made and received for transactions carried out across national boundaries' (1). This sub-order is closely connected with the rules for international trade. Another order — the patent system, as it was laid down in the Paris Convention of 1883 — is on the other hand almost fairly independent. It can be amended without affecting the rest of the international rules. There are also some orders — e.g. the 'oil order' or the 'shipping order' — which are to a large extent determined by private corporations.

The definition we have chosen relates to the rules of the game in force. It is, of course, obvious that there is often a difference between formal rules and actual practice. The treatment of dependent developing countries by the major powers is one example. The IMF's decisions, rules and general practice have constituted the formal framework for the monetary cooperation of the Western world during the postwar period, but the actual decisions have nearly always been taken by a smaller group of rich countries. Most of the developing countries belong to GATT, but it has hitherto been generally accepted that they can diverge from the current rules. There are also rules that are applied but are not accepted. In the maritime sphere the shipping companies decide within so-called liner conferences what freight standards are applied. Most of the developing countries oppose this cartellisation of the market, but they do not yet have the power to change the prevailing order.

The prevailing world order reflects the balance of power in the world. It was chiefly the United States that elaborated and introduced the present rules. And it is only the rich countries that have in a real sense participated in and influenced discussions about changes. Power also decides the conditions for participation. In the summer of 1973 the United States could stop exports of soya beans to Japan, despite the agreements entered into, because no retaliatory measures were feared (2). During the dollar crises the EEC did not succeed in forcing the

United States to pursue a 'responsible' economic policy. The world order is quite simply a system of penalties and rewards that rests on the prevailing power structure. Each country tries to weigh the advantages of obeying the rules against the disadvantages of breaking them. It is obvious that the risks for small dependent developing countries are extremely high (3). The United States' blockade of Cuba is an example. The World Bank and IMF have taken it upon themselves to enforce the rules *vis-a-vis* many countries over the years (4). The EEC recently 'punished' Sweden's import restrictions on shoes by restricting its own imports of paper.

It is simply impossible to establish a system of rules that diverges significantly from the economic interests of the major powers. The United States and the EEC would never, for example, participate in a monetary system in which the UN General Assembly decided the amount of international liquidity to be created.

It is obvious that the developing countries, in working towards the NIEO, do not simply want to get new rules adopted. They want simultaneously to extend the formal system of rules to cover new areas. An example of this is their proposal to ban all forms of bilateral pressures. They also want to extend the system of rules as it refers to transnational corporations and the transfer of technical know-how.

The debate concerns — at least formally — a new international economic order. In practice it is about the rules of the game played by rich and poor market economies — and the negotiations concern primarily the relations *between* these two *groups* of countries.

The Swedish poet Lars Forssell, in one of his poems, gave the advice: 'never say that you are a communist/like a billion others' — but it should be remembered that one third of the world's population lives in a state-controlled order of its own. The governments of their countries have no intention of exchanging it for another. It is therefore possible to talk of two world orders; but it seems more correct to say that the communist countries participate in the capitalist world order on special terms.

In order to put some meat on these rather abstract bones

— let us see how many economic world orders we can distinguish during the last 300–400 years. We have mercantilism — nationalistic, export-oriented, strictly regulated and still permeated with the Jewish–Christian ethics of the middle ages. During the eighteenth century liberalism advances. The belief in an international exchange of commodities becomes established. Ethics are thrown overboard. Man is selfish and must be so. The just price — which has been a preoccupation of earlier philosophers and economists — is settled by the world order. It functions up to the Great War, is passably restored by the 1920s, only to collapse after the stock market crash of 1929 in a tangle of bilateral agreements. Finally we have the world order described in Chapter 2 which was established after the Second World War.

Only two of these orders can be termed, in any real sense, functioning international order — the one preceding the Great War and the one that appeared after the Second World War. And they have one feature in common that is worth noting. They were both 'managed' by a single dominant country, Great Britain and the United States respectively. What we are now seeking, whether we want it or not, is a more democratic order — and the core of the problem is the force that can hold such an order together (4).

IS THERE A PROPOSAL FOR A NEW WORLD ORDER?

There is no detailed proposal for new rules for the world economy or for the relations between rich and poor market economies.

Only on a few points do the recommendations of the Sixth Special Session of the General Assembly indicate in clear terms what measures are required. The industrialised countries are thus urged to lower their tariffs on imports from the developing contries and to grant official aid corresponding to 0.7 per cent of their GNP. Most of the other recommendations urge the rich countries in general terms to take steps to improve the situation of the developing countries in various spheres.

In the case of the developing countries' production of

foodstuffs, for example, there is a recommendation that the international efforts concerning the food problems (shall) 'take full account of special problems of developing countries, particularly in times of food shortages'. Most of the recommendations under the heading 'Food', with the exception of the traditional aid demands, are about equally vague. Nowhere is it clearly spelled out which 'special problems' are to be given priority and which of the endeavours of the developing countries are particularly important.

Under the heading 'General Trade' there is an exhortation to prepare 'an overall integrated programme . . . for a comprehensive range of commodities of export interest to developing countries'. The programme should provide guidelines and in that connection take 'into account the current work in this field'. It is undoubtedly a gigantic task. But nothing more is said about the programme than that it shall 'provide guidelines', which appears to be a minimum demand.

When it comes to the transfer of technology it is proposed, inter alia, that international rules should be drawn up 'for the transfer of technology corresponding to the needs and conditions prevalent in developing countries' and that the developing countries should be given access to modern technology 'on improved terms'.

In the case of the international monetary system, it is suggested that it should check inflation and contribute to stabilising the world economy. Everyone agrees on this, but nobody knows how to do it.

On some points the text of the action programme is clearer. Thus with regard to the developing countries' debt burden it states that new negotiations should commence 'with a view to concluding agreements on debt cancellation, moratorium, rescheduling or interest subsidisation' (5).

These quotations from the Programme of Action do not aim to ridicule the UN or to reduce the significance of the agreements. A voluminous text which has been compromised into shape in a race against time, with 50–60 countries represented by active delegates, is always easy to criticise. The purpose of the very few selected quotations is only to show that much work remains to be done before we can talk of a complete

Programme of Action to establish a new international economic order.

The representatives of the group of developing countries are naturally quite clear about that. One of the leading representatives of a developing country during the negotiations in recent years, the former Iranian Minister of the Interior, Jahangir Amuzegar, aptly called the UN recommendations a proposal for a 'new deal' rather than a 'new order' (6). Venezuela's Manuel Perez-Guerrero, former Secretary General of UNCTAD, stated in a speech two years ago that 'the resolution of the General Assembly was only a step, even if it was an important one, in a process which has taken several years to mature'. And now we are at the 'starting point' for the planning of NIEO (7).

Despite all the obscurities there have been several ambitious attempts to interpret the UN texts in various political directions. Some believe that the recommendations from the Sixth Special Session of the UN General Assembly aim at a kind of international planned economy. This view is based on the fact that some of the proposals suggest the need for considerable market intervention. Others read the texts as a recommendation for continued capitalist growth and, in so doing, base their remarks on what is said about liberalising trade, capital movements and other transactions. In the first spate of enthusiasm some groups also imagined that the UN resolution embodied a plan for a world society that would economise more with non-renewable resources. These expectations, however, find little support in the adopted texts.

The first two readings are possible, however — and following on from them a third variant, namely one that asserts that some of the proposals, even in their present imprecise formulation, appear to be irreconcilable.

Summarising drastically, but not altogether unfairly, one can say that the Sixth Special Session of the General Assembly recommends an integrated, though not yet fully spelled-out programme to give the developing countries a larger share of the world's resources and power. This is meant to take place by means of continued rapid economic growth within a framework for a stabilised and liberalised world economy. In other words simply, as Amuzegar pointed out, a 'new deal' for the poor countries in the world. It is thus not a matter of new and different world order. The demands of the developing countries are really quite modest.

One can also distinguish between short-term demands and more fundamental aims in the UN resolution. Thus short-term objectives are the individual demands for such things as aid, stable prices and tariff preferences. These proposals are, however, circumscribed by a philosophy that aims to strengthen the collective influence of the developing countries over the world economy. What the developing countries seek to achieve is, among other things, an international system of rules that legitimises their attempts to nationalise foreign-owned enterprises and to strengthen their political sovereignty.

It should finally be added that it is still mainly a matter of demands supported only by the developing countries. As early as 1974 the majority of the industrialised countries expressed their doubts in so-called explanations of vote. During the last 3–4 years the majority within the group of industrialised countries has shown with increasing clarity that it does not share the developing countries' conception of what changes are possible or desirable.

HOW DOES A NEW WORLD ORDER COME INTO BEING?

The negotiations about the NIEO at the Seventh Special Session of the General Assembly in the autumn of 1975 came gradually to be concentrated to a few smaller negotiation groups. These had to 'sew up' the last compromises before the resolution could be adopted. A Swedish morning paper referred to 'selected groups that decided what kind of economic order the world is to have in the future' (8).

The truth was, of course, that the task of the groups was to draft formulas which might just be acceptable to the rich countries.

But how is a new economic order decided upon and brought into being? Shall we get a new international economic order as a result of the UN's recommendations? This question is dealt with by Marian Radetzki in his book *A New International Economic Order* and he answers it as follows:

'In the short term, say until the end of the this decade, the answer is . . . probably no. The readiness of the industrialised countries to accede to the varying demands of the third world is . . . virtually non-existent. And the developing countries are at present too divided and incapable of taking a forceful common stand' (9).

Only towards the end of this century does Radetzki believe that 'we shall experience rather revolutionary changes in the relations between rich and poor countries which will correct the present imbalance' (9).

This appears at first sight to be an unquestionable argument. But it overlooks something essential. The world order is in a constant state of change. The set of rules for international trade has evolved gradually during the postwar period. The monetary system has changed radically several times during the twentieth century. During the postwar period alone one can speak of two or more international monetary systems. In talking of the existing international economic order it should therefore be clear that this has not been one and the same even during the postwar period — and that it will change during the remainder of the century irrespective of the decisions taken at the UN.

There are many indications that an era has just begun in which the changes will occur with particular rapidity. The justification for talking of a new, and not just an altered world order is largely a question of nuances, value judgements and perspectives. Decolonisation and the simultaneous liberation of China from foreign influence may have signified a new order. The previously dominant position of the United States in the world economy has gradually been undermined. The oil crisis meant, among other things, that the big oil companies no longer fix the price of energy by themselves. At the same time the power of the OPEC countries grew. Is this sufficient to allow us to talk of a new world order or is it only a question of important changes within the existing system? The answer to that question depends on what one means by NIEO. Is it a question of new rules for cooperation between states or is it enough to achieve a more equitable distribution of power and resources within the present order? Whatever reply one gives to this question it should be borne in mind that hardly any of the changes that have occurred so far have benefitted the earth's poorest countries.

We should also realise that it will not be a case of arriving at one single collective decision to introduce a new international economic order. The various proposals that were put forward at the Sixth Special Session of the General Assembly will be discussed in numerous expert and study groups, at conferences and meetings under the auspices of various international organisations. Some of the proposals will become outdated before this work is brought to a conclusion. Other questions will get stuck in the negotiating machinery because the countries are unable to reach agreement. In some cases, however, the proposals are likely to be formulated in such a way that they will become acceptable additions to the international system. How or when this happens will depend on the economic trend and the relative positions of power of the groups of countries which, in their turn, influence the international 'negotiation climate'. It is an open question whether the sum of these successive additions to and changes in the rules of the game will eventually lead us to talk of a new international order.

As we have already indicated, revolutionary changes in the world economy are taking place while the NIEO debate is still in progress. A number of developing countries are engaged in winning an increased share of the world trade in industrial products. The professional competence of the developing countries when it comes to negotiation with industrialised countries and transnational corporations is steadily growing. Negotiations at the UN should deal with how much and in which direction we should guide developments resulting from changes in the productive forces throughout the world. This may appear to be an excessively limited aim, but this work is important because current development is having an adverse effect on really poor people in various countries.

What is happening right now is that we are in transition from a formerly strict hierarchical world, with the United States as its undisputed leader, to an order 'in which nobody is responsible'

(10). According to the American political scientist Robert W. Tucker it is not only the case that the predominant position of the United States has been undermined. At the same time military methods of exercising power have become less applicable. This constitutes a problem according to Tucker — who won world notoriety by suggesting an occupation of the oil fields in Western Asia during the oil crisis — as military measures may be very precise, while economic sanctions are rather blunt intruments (11).

What sort of order do the developing countries wish to substitute for the existing one, then? How will a new order function and what will keep it together?

Several leading spokesman of the developing countries clearly envisage a world order based on growing yet more equitable interdependence between the countries of the world (12). The cohesive force in such an order must evidently be the positive interest of all countries in following the rules of the game. According to Jagdish Bhagwati this may come about, for instance, through mutually advantageous commercial treaties and the joint administration of the resources of the seabed (13). Presumably one must also envisage the possibility of fairly strict collective sanctions.

But is it feasible to separate power and formal rules to the extent that this presupposes? Is it not the case, as Benjamin Watkins Leigh expressed it over a century ago, that 'power and poverty may be separated for a time by force or fraud — but divorced, never. For so soon as the pain of separation is felt . . . property will purchase power, or power will take over property' (14).

And Perez-Guerrero, too, has pointed out that 'the law has never been in the vanguard for progress . . . it has always reflected the balance of power in any given society at a given point of time' (15).

The truth, unfortunately, is probably that the emancipation of the developing countries — like that of the working-class — must in the main be their own doing. A redistribution of the world's resources will not come about 'by mere talk', as an Iraqi delegate put it at the General Assembly of 1975 (16). No ruling class has ever voluntarily relinquished its privileges. And it is significant of the situation of the developing countries that, at the UN in the spring of 1974, they requested assistance to 'facilitate the functioning and to further the aims of the producers' associations' — they asked for permission to do what OPEC had done on its own initiative.

It is a dismal conclusion. But it is not devoid of hope. The growing interdependence of the states of the world, on which the developing countries base their expectations, is a reality. The main problem, as the chairman of the OECD's Development Assistance Committee has pointed out, is how we can 'handle the increasing mutual interdependence' (17). Nor do we believe, and we shall later try to demonstrate this, that the developing countries have exhausted or even seriously exploited their resources of power.* It should also be possible to bring about significant changes within the world order which is now emerging.

We should add here, however, that the growing international disorder now evident is not principally a question of interstate relations. The unwillingness or incapacity of the states to adhere to the established rules has national causes. The world order that prevailed before the Great War was an affair of the upper class. In all the major countries a small elite with a strong interest in international trade controlled a large part of the economic surplus. The functioning international order of the postwar period was attended by a rapid growth of production. This made it possible, at least in the industrialised countries, to provide a higher real standard of living for all groups in society. Now powerful organised interests confront each other in the struggle for shares of a pie that is no longer increasing. Previously jobs that had been rationalised out of existence could be replaced by new ones in expanding branches of industry. The rich countries now face the threat of an actual decrease in the number of productive jobs.

---

* See p. 167 et seq. for a discussion about a possible new negotiation strategy for developing countries.

A CRITICAL LOOK AT SOME CENTRAL DEMANDS OF THE DEVELOPING COUNTRIES

It is important to define what we mean by the demands of the developing countries in this section. In the first place they amount to proposals put forward by the governments of the developing countries. Secondly they are demands on which over a hundred governments have been able to agree.

The demands of the developing countries are usually formuated at special meetings of the developing countries which precede UN or UNCTAD conferences. Even if only 20–30 developing countries have active interests in several spheres, it goes without saying that it is extremely difficult for the developing countries to establish clear priorities among the various demands during a few hectic conference sessions. For that reason the addition method is usually employed. As the demands that are advanced are usually directed to the industrialised countries and are virtually never assumed to involve negative effects for any developing country, each participating state can add its desired aims to the common list. Occasionally even mutually incompatible demands may be included on the same list of desiderata.

Consequently the demands of the developing countries are usually both extensive and detailed. But this common list makes the position of the developing countries extremely rigid when they get down to negotiations at a conference. It is very difficult to make tactical dispositions during the course of a conference, as this would require that priority be given to proposals which are of particular importance to certain countries. As a result it is to a certain degree the industrialised countries that do the priority grading of the demands of the developing countries. The negotiations are concentrated to the areas where there appears to be a chance that the industrialised countries will accept some concessions.

This negotiation method of the developing countries inevitably lead to their putting forward certain ill-advised proposals. Sometimes the proposals may be unnecessarily complicated or elaborate in relation to the problem in hand and/or to alternative solutions. Guarantees to maintain the value of the developing countries' currency reserves would seem to belong to this category. In other instances proposals may possibly have negative effects on the developing countries themselves. Also that some of the demands of the developing countries may, of course, be regarded as morally unjustified. They may be demands from the governments of the developing countries — and these do not directly represent the interests of the people in all developing countries. We shall return to this question later on.

It is easy to find some peripheral demands of developing countries which appear to be ill-advised or unnecessarily complicated. Here, however, we shall — even in a very preliminary fashion — look at some of the central demands of the developing countries: indexation, stabilisation of prices and revenues, the integrated commodity programme, the code of conduct for liner conferences, and debt cancellation.

Another factor that has determined this selection is that both aims and means must be stated with a degree of clarity that makes it possible to analyse them in a meaningful way. The developing countries' claim for 25 per cent of the world's industry by the year 2000 is a central aim, but the means for attaining this aim are not specific enough to be analysed.

Another demand of the developing countries which we do not examine involves the demand for a new monetary order. The desire for a monetary system that will provide increased stability and lower inflation is shared by the group of developing countries with all the government of industrialised countries. The problem is that nobody knows what form such a system should take. And that is not surprising. The monetary system is largely a reflection of the prevailing instability of the world economy. To make it possible to return to a system of fixed exchange rates the minimum requirement is that the leading industrial countries should accept coordination of financial and monetary policies. If, for example, the currency of one country weakens, the government must intervene and pursue a restrictive economic policy which restricts imports and strengthens international competitiveness. A country with a particularly rapid development of productivity must pursue an expansive policy and permit a rise in real wages to prevent the currency from becoming too strong. It is not possible to achieve stability in the world economy by means of a new monetary system. One can only have a stable monetary system if the world economy is already stable.

We have thus chosen to deal with some demands of the developing countries which are important and at the same time possible to analyse.

Indexation and deteriorating terms of trade

By indexation is meant measures to achieve a just and equitable relationship between the prices of primary commodities manufactured and semi-manufactured goods exported by developing countries and the price of primary commodities, manufactures capital goods and equipment imported by them.

The purpose of indexation is to prevent the developing countries from being forced to export an ever larger amount of primary commodities in order to buy a given quantity of industrial products.

In the advanced era in which we live we should not reject any proposal on the grounds of technical difficulty. We would simply remark that indexation is a rather complicated and bureaucratic way of dealing with a problem for which there are other, simpler solutions. If, in fact, it should even be regarded as an inter-state problem?

The question of the developing countries' terms of trade *vis-a-vis* the rest of the world — what they have to pay for imports as compared to what they are paid for exports — is rightly a central one in the debate about development. The changes of the terms of trade is a pure gain, while an increase in exports can only come about as a result of increased inputs of productive resources.

The view of the group of developing countries on these questions is strongly coloured by the theory evolved by UNCTAD's first Secretary General, Raul Prebisch. The central argument in Prebisch's theory, specifically evolved for the Latin American countries, is that the terms of trade for the primary commodity exports of the developing countries are deteriorating in the long term. The reason is that the gains in productivity occurring in the industrialised countries — which ought to lead to lowered prices — remain in these countries because of strong trade unions with high pay claims. But the gains in productivity in the developing countries are transferred to the consumers in the industrialised countries. Other elements of the theory are that the demand for primary commodities grows slowly, partly because of the increasing use of synthetic materials and the more effective utilisation of natural raw materials (18). Hans Singer extended the theory by pointing out that the extraction of minerals in the developing countries is often in the hands of transnational corporations, which means that the diffusion effects are small (19).

When these theories were formulated they seemed to rest on solid empirical ground. A considerable deterioration in the terms of trade of the developing countries and raw materials had, as we have shown above, occurred in the 1950s.* There was also a widespread opinion, based on two UN reports (20), that the prices of primary commodities in relation to the prices of manufactured goods had deteriorated by not less than 43 per cent from the last 25 years of the nineteenth century until the Great War.

The deterioration during the 1950s was of short duration — it occurred chiefly during the period 1954–62 — and represented a downward adjustment of the high primary commodity prices of the Korean boom. The trend up to the Great War is more interesting. A Belgian economist Paul Bairoch, has recently done something as unusual as plodding back to the original source material — and in doing so has reached quite different conclusions from those of the UN studies. Bairoch mentions three main sources of error. The UN index for exports of manufactured goods is based entirely on British exports and the assumption that this provides an average for prices on industrial products throughout the world. This assumption turns out to be mistaken and the differences are great. Secondly, the index for prices of primary commodities is based on Great Britain's wholesale prices index for those products. It turns out that the British prices rose more slowly than in the rest of the world.

* See p. 54 et seq.

The third source of error lies in the inclusion of 100 per cent of the costs of freight and insurance in the case of primary commodity prices, while the proportion of these in the prices for industrial products is only 50 per cent. This means that the very large reductions in freight rates and insurance premiums have been entered as part of the fall in raw material prices to a disproportionate extent. Bairoch's conclusion is that the terms of trade for primary commodities *improved* by 20–40 per cent from the end of the 1870s to the end of the 1920s (21).

It would appear that the thesis of constantly falling raw material prices is not so much a theory as a misunderstanding of reality. But there is still a proposal for indexation and the question is whether this will *in future* favour producers of primary commodites.*

It is naturally difficult to have a definite opinion on how the prices of a number of commodity groups will develop. In the case of food prices, for example, there are diametrically opposed views (22), between which we are unable to make a judgement. But let us hazard some guesses about the prices for other primary commodities and manufactured goods. Several factors indicate that the relative prices of primary commodities will improve. Within the mining industries the most accessible sources of raw materials are likely to be in production now. Costs may therefore be expected to rise. On the other hand the output of synthetic products will probably continue to have a moderating effect on prices for such commodities as sisal, cotton, jute and rubber. In the case of industrial products it seems likely that a growing proportion of the gains in productivity will have to be surrendered to the purchasers, partly as a result of the rapidly increasing competition from countries with cheap labour. It is, of course, true that transnational corporations are in a strong position in many developing countries. But these enterprises are drawn mainly to markets dominated by a small number of firms where oligopoly profits are to be gained. They therefore avoid markets where they meet price competition, and this is the weapon used by national

---

* The question of who benefits from high prices of primary commodities is dealt with in the section 'International and national problems'.

enterprises in developing countries and by transnational enterprises based in such countries (23). In Japan there are already advanced plans to restructure the economy towards an increasingly advanced technology output and to leave the price-squeezed traditional production to developing countries in Asia.

Our conclusion is therefore that the terms of trade of non-edible primary commodities in relation to manufactured goods may well improve as a result of economic development. At all events, indexation appears to be an unnecessarily complicated system when profits are so uncertain. One must also identify the developing countries which will gain and those which will lose before going any further.

The integrated commodity programme — stabilisation of prices and export revenues

The integrated commodity programme is according to Perez-Guerrero 'the very corner stone of the programme which constitutes the NIEO' (24). This programme aims to reduce the fluctuations in price and supply of a number of primary commodities and to maintain prices that are equitable for consumers and remurative for producers. These objectives are to be reached, inter alia by means of

(a) international buffer stocks which buy when prices are low and sell when they are high;
(b) a common fund to finance the buffer stocks;
(c) multilateral commodity agreements;
(d) improved compensatory financing to assist countries whose export revenues suddenly decline.

The element of integration in the programme consists primarily in the fact that it embraces several primary commodities and is financed through a common fund. The proposal is not included in the UN resolution on NIEO of 1974 — but the ideas about a unified programme, stability and remunerative prices are there. The integrated commodity programme was elaborated within the secretariat of UNCTAD and was the main subject at that organisation's conference in Nairobi in 1976.

The idea of stabilising prices and markets is not a new one. The thought of an integrated programme has been alive within the UNCTAD secretariat since it was established. As we have shown earlier, as far back as at the Bandung Conference, the developing countries demanded 'collective measures'.* The proposal for supplementary financing** played a key role from the first UNCTAD conference and for several years subsequently; and a desire for a stable world order permeates the whole UN resolution on NIEO. Generally speaking, it can be said that a dominating theme in the strategy of the developing countries during the postwar period has been an attempt to stabilise and regulate the world around them.

We shall therefore not discuss the specific proposal for an integrated programme but instead focus on some of the methods that are important in all stabilisation arrangements.

In order to do so we have to keep some problems separate which should preferably not be 'integrated':

(a) Is it a matter of a covert transfer of resources or only of stabilising prices? For all arrangements in this sphere it is necessary to estimate at what long-term level prices should be held. It is natural that the developing countries will want to maintain a fairly high price level in order to gain as much income as possible. If one merely aims at levelling out the fluctuations in the price level, the developing countries will not be paid more in the long run.*** There are two quite distinct problems, however. The first is an attempt to transfer real resources. The second refers to technical possibilities for stabilising prices at a level that is reasonable from a market point of view.

(b) It is prices or export revenues that are to be stabilised? Can both prices and export revenues be stablised at the same time?

Let us first assume that when the developing countries talk of 'remunerative' prices for the producers they mean higher prices. They thus wish to use the stabilisation arrangements to achieve

*   See pp. 87-88.
**   See p. 62.
*** See however below, pp. 139-170.

a transfer of resources.

The question then arises what is the advantage of taking this roundabout route via the integrated commodity programme. There are much simpler and more direct methods. The only 'advantage'* we can see is that consumer countries will not have to finance this transfer of resources through taxes — the burden will be directly off-loaded into the consumers. It will thus become a regressive tax that hits the poorest groups hardest. This form of transfer of resources will thereby contribute to increase the income and wealth disparities in all importing countries, to which the developing countries also belong. It is possible, however, that this kind of stabilisation arrangement is a simpler method of obtaining increased resources than through the traditional aid to those countries which export large quantities of attractive raw materials.

But why should these countries in particular or the enterprises in such countries receive increased resources? 'The stabilisation method' implies that one decides at random to give increased aid to those countries which are producing primary commodities, the prices of which can be kept at a high level. Why those countries in particular? — they already have the advantage of being able to sell attractive primary commodities.

Another problem in using price stabilisation as a method of transferring resources is that most primary commodities are exported by industrialised countries and developing countries as well as by countries of the Eastern bloc and are purchased by many countries. It is thus a very imprecise method with a high degree of leakage as compared with aid.

Attempts to maintain a high price level must probably be complemented by agreements to limit production. This is usually done by distributing the total planned export between the exporting countries by means of quotas. The effects on the income distribution of this will be dealt with in a later section.

High prices tend to encourage increased production. All

* One should not disregard the fact, however, that this may actually be an advantage. In certain countries it may be easier for the government to let the consumers pay for the transfer of resources through higher prices rather than to increase the aid budget.

countries with regulated agricultural prices know that. But the chances of maintaining an artificial price level are thereby reduced. The buffer stock is forced to buy more and more and sell less and less. And if the money runs out, the bottom falls out of the market entirely.

Is it in the developing countries' own interest to encourage new investments in mineral extraction and primary commodities production by means of stabilised, higher prices? It seems more reasonable instead to concentrate investments in primary commodities creating an automatic rise in prices. In the long term there is not much different between the two alternatives — they both lead to higher prices. But the latter method still appears to be superior. It is simpler. The exporting countries only have to agree on export quotas, and that they must do by the stabilisation method as well. No resources have to be deposited in funds but can instead be used for industrial investments. There is no risk of large price-cutting sales from ruined buffer stocks. The risk that higher prices will cause consumers to switch to buying substitutes is equally great in both cases, but costs less in the latter.

It was strategy advocated here that Kissinger was worried about when he put forward a proposal at the UNCTAD conference at Nairobi in 1976 for an international resources bank to finance investments to increase the production of primary commodities in the developing countries. The present lending policy of the World Bank also aims to help safeguard supplies of cheap raw materials to the industrialised countries.

We must add here, however, that several sources report that the transnational corporations are increasingly directing their prospecting for raw materials towards countries outside the third world (25). If this endeavour produces results in the form of resources that can be extracted at competitive prices, the whole question of the transfer of resources by means of higher prices will be put in a new light.

Are today's raw material prices just? This question was a very central one in antiquity and the middle ages for the philosophers who occupied themselves with economic questions. Thomas Aquinas — who had ideas about everything — regarded the just price as that which permitted the seller to maintain his accustomed way of life. Nothing must be allowed to disturb the divinely ordered social hierarchy. We may assume that this great preserver of status quo would also have accepted the injustices of today (26). Eventually this and several other questions of justice disappeared from the agenda of political economy. As early as the eighteenth century it was seen that competition — as the Finno–Swedish clergyman and economist Anders Chydenius put it — 'weighs everyone in the same balance, and profit is the right measure, showing to whom the advantage should fall' (27).

For the sake of argument, however, and without laying claim to blazing new philosophical trails, let us here agree with Perez-Guerrero 'that it is difficult to decide what is an equitable price . . . but you know when it is inequitable'. Let us therefore assume that the prices for the developing countries' primary commodities are inequitably low. But — even if we exclude oil — there are many that earn big money on raw materials.

The issue of equitable price must presumably be linked to the way in which export incomes are distributed between those who own the mines and plantations and those who mine the ore and pick the coffee. If prices are to be raised in order to achieve global equity, one must really both keep that distribution in mind and also, as far as possible, distinguish between primary commodities produced by small farmers and those produced on large plantations (28).

It is obviously simpler to stabilise the price around the level established by the market. Provided that one finds the right price, the purchases and sales of the buffer stocks should balance each other. But what is the point of stabilising the price if one does not gain anything from it? Low incomes remain low incomes even if they are stable, as the Pakistani economist Mahbub ul Haq has pointed out (29).

It is not certain, however, that price stabilisation at the level established by the market would signify unaltered incomes for all exporting countries. In order to buy and sell at the right moment in a market where prices change rapidly, one needs expertise. It seems probable that the industrialised countries have information about markets which is both more accurate and up-to-date than that of the developing countries.

In addition, the groups of buyers and sellers in the United States, Japan and Europe are often able to influence the market to their advantage. This might support the argument that most developing countries do in fact gain from stable prices. Furthermore price stabilisation should involve savings in real resources if production planning is facilitated so that available productive resources are utilised more effectively. If we take just one developing country it is possible that a stabilised price, together with a buffer stock of some major export commodity, could, on the one hand, facilitate production planning and, on the other, held to allocate administrative resources to other areas.

Unstable prices are a symptom. But what is their cause? This we must know so that price stabilisation does not have the wrong effect. Are the price fluctuations due to changes in demand or to variations in the quantity supplied? If the instability is a result of changing demand, most of the evidence would indicate that stable prices reduce incomes for the exporting countries. The profits go to the importers. If variations in supply cause the price fluctuations, the exporters will probably gain. It is possible, however, that stable prices will lead to more unstable export revenues. Let us assume that changes in price and supply previously cancelled each other out; i.e. when the supply was low because of frost in the coffee-growing regions of Brazil, the price was raised and the sum of price multiplied by quantity remained unchanged. But if the price is quite stable, then all variations in the supply will have a full impact and destabilise export revenues. This problem is particularly acute for those countries that are major exporters of a certain commodity. Only when both demand and supply have a sufficiently low price elasticity* (less than 1) does price stabilisation lead to stabler export revenues in a market where fluctuations are caused by variations in supply.

---

* Elasticity is a measure of, for example, the responsiveness of demand to a change in price. If the price is reduced by 10 per cent and thereby causes an increase in demand of more than 10 per cent, this is referred to as a demand elasticity that is greater than 1. The result will be that the overall income increases. Whether the profit for the seller increases is, of course, quite another matter. Economists generally hold that the conditions mentioned in the text are fulfilled only to the case of a few commodities. The developing countries themselves have a more optimistic view of the elasticity of various raw materials.

There is an extensive literature on the subject of price stabilisation that we cannot deal with here more than to say that economists are in fairly general agreement that price stabilisation is a rather problematic method and that the gains for the exporting countries are uncertain (30).

The reasonable aim must, of course, be to stabilise a country's overall export revenues* — not what is earned from a single commodity. This outlook was the basis for the previously mentioned proposal for supplementary financing. The plan depended on a reasonable forecast of future export revenues being establised for all participating developing countries. If revenues fell below the anticipated level — due to unforeseen circumstances — the country would receive compensation from a fund.

This all seems very reasonable. All investigations that have been made show that export revenues for most developing countries are far more unstable than those of the industrialised countries. How can a poor country plan its economic development if the government does not know approximately how much money will be earned from exports? It is that revenue which will pay for a large part of the imports needed for development.

The problem is simply that it has not been possible to prove a clear correlation between fluctuating export revenues and negative effects in the exporting countries. Despite many and extensive studies there is just no evidence that fluctuations in export revenues affect savings, investments and economic growth in a negative direction. On the contrary the correlations which have been noted indicate the reverse. Thus Alasdair MacBean found a positive correlation between the instability of export revenues and the growth of investments; the greater the variations in export revenues, the larger the proportion of GNP was saved and invested (31). In the latest major study of these questions Knudsen and Parnes found that savings, investments and economic growth were positively correlated with

* It is really all revenues, i.e. export revenues, tourist revenues and other capital flows, as well as capital flows, that should be stablised. We restrict ourselves here to discussing the proposals for stabilising export revenues which, after all, for most developing countries are the dominant item of income.

instability (32). And Kreinin and Finger maintained that 'export earnings stability is a *luxury* for government officials who manage foreign accounts, not a *necessity* in the development process (33).

The positive correlation between high instability and a high investment quota may be a coincidence. Yet it is interesting that this tallies with the permanent income hyopthesis in economics. A person is expected to save a smaller proportion of his basic income than of occasional extra earnings. So the larger the unforeseen extra earnings are the greater is the amount saved.

Whether this behaviour can be applied to a nation's economy is doubtful. It does not seem unlikely, however, that several developing countries may start extensive investment programmes when export revenues are high and raise loans when there is an unforeseen export shortfall. This might explain the positive correlation that several studies have demonstrated. In that case, however, the problems have in part merely been postponed — for the debts must be repaid. Another explanation may be that a large proportion of imports and exports are handled by large enterprises — national and transnational — which are loosely integrated in the economy of the country. The investment plans of such enterprises may not be affected by temporary fluctuations and a reduction in income mainly takes the form of a simultaneous decrease in repatriated profits and other capital outflows. In order to study the connection between export instability and economic development in a meaningful way, one should probably investigate how the export sector is integrated in the economy of a country, how the national budget is affected and whose incomes increase or decrease. When Mossadeq nationalised the oil companies in Iran and the export of oil virtually ceased because of the boycott by Great Britain and the United States, the broad masses of the people were surprisingly little affected. The Anglo Persian Oil Company was largely a foreign enclave which imported nearly all that it needed, including labour and sand, and the limited revenues which the company's book-keeping allotted to the Iranian state remained in the pockets of a small elite (34). For Sri Lanka, Ghana and Tanzania the economic consequences will be quite different if there is a sharp drop in the prices of tea, cocoa and sisal.

Considering our lack of precise knowledge, we should perhaps refrain from general conclusions. It is possible that the proposal for revenue stabilisation will justify its place on the international agenda. But there is no strong evidence that it is an economically sound proposition to invest money in stabilising export revenues.

UNCTAD's code of conduct for liner conferences

In 1974 a code of conduct for liner conferences for international maritime traffic, elaborated within UNCTAD, was adopted at an international conference. Several industrial countries voted with the developing countries for the code. It will only come into force, however, two years after it has been ratified by at least 24 countries that also represent 25 per cent of the world's shipping tonnage. This goal is still far away. Like all other countries with a large merchant fleet of its own, Sweden voted against the proposal.

The aim of the code is to divide up the freight traffic so that the importing country carries 40 per cent, the exporting country the same amount, and only 20 per cent is left free for other countries to compete for. If one of the countries in a bilateral trade exchange cannot handle its 40 per cent, this proportion of the market is transferred to the other country.

One might, of course, ask what is so special about this particular sector. Why should not all countries manufacture a certain proportion of all computers, private cars and TV sets that are sold? The explanation is simple. Maritime freight traffic of a cartel ridden market which the developing countries regards as flagrantly unfair. The freight rates are determined by the major shipping lines at liner conferences. The cost of transporting goods between two developing countries on the same continent is nearly always higher than the freight rate to New York, London or Rotterdam. The liner conferences simply extract the rates the market will bear and the developing countries have no other recourse than the shipping conferences dominated by the industrialised countries (35). There is also a study indicating that the structure of the freight rates can counteract the efforts of developing countries to process their own raw materials (36). Today 60 per cent of freight volume is taken on board in developing countries, but the latter own only 7 per cent of the merchant fleet, if we exclude Liberia and Panama.

Attempts to regulate maritime trade are by no means new. England introduced the Navigation Act in 1651* in order to limit the competition from the more effective Dutch shipping companies. The system was retained, however, when Great Britain had established itself as the world's leading maritime nation, and was only abolished in 1849. In 1724, Sweden enacted its 'Produce Edict' to ban any foreign ships from unloading any goods other than those shipped by its own country.

The developing countries can thus refer to both a fully justified criticism of the international shipping market and to historical parallels. But is the proposed code a good solution?

In the long run the code could probably increase revenues for shipping companies in the developing countries — private, nationalised and foreign-owned. In the short run, however, it is mainly developed countries with a merchant fleet of adequate size that will benefit. The shipping companies in those countries can handle 40 per cent of their own country's trade with the rest of the world and an even larger share of the trade with developing countries before the latter have been able to build up their own shipping companies. Among the most favoured countries are the United States and West Germany. And as it is a case of monopoly markets, one result will undoubtedly be a general rise in freight rates. The costs of the American shipping companies in particular are, despite state subsidies, very high. One sign of this is the sky-high freight rates charged on aid deliveries tied to American shipping.

It is possible of course to argue against all kinds of tariffs and regulations. But it is an inescapable fact that all industrial activity has started with the support of tariff protection and/or

---

* The Navigation Act gave English shipping companies a monopoly on all trade to and from England and its colonies with the exception that a nation that exported its own products could ship these in its own vessels to England. The Navigation Act had been written much earlier, but had not then been enforceable.

subsidies. This was also true of British industry, which was protected from Indian exports of cotton textiles. If the developing countries are to be able to build up their shipping industry rapidly, this must be supported. And even if direct subsidies are often more effective and fair, navigation acts may be the second best and only feasible solution.

But the sensible solution − if we accept the above argument − is to protect only the developing countries' share of the trade. This share should in that case be set at the level which the shipping companies of the developing countries can handle today and then gradually be raised. All developing countries would in fact benefit from this. Profits will be the same, but the price of services bought from outside will be lower. Even if the shipping conferences continue to exist, they are preferable to regular monopolies. The adjustment of the maritime nations to the increasing market share of the developing countries will be relatively painless (37). Others will have to worry about the problems of German and American shipowners.

Debt cancellation

The developing countries' deficits in the balance of trade and on current accounts have always been prominent in the warning reports issued from time to time. The truth is that neither deficits nor the debt burden were a general problem before the crisis of the mid-1970s. Assertions that growing deficits in the balance of trade were a serious problem of the developing countries before 1973 were empirically unwarranted as well as theoretically wrong.

Poor countries have − we hope −·more ambitious investment programmes than they can finance with current export revenues. They must receive aid or borrow money in order to be able to increase imports. This causes the balance of trade to go into deficit. This is precisely what Sweden, the United States, Canada, Australia and several other countries did before the Great War, and this is what developing countries want and ought to do today. Large deficits in the balance of trade are thus theoretically correct and, as long as the investments that are financed with borrowed money increase productive capacity at a faster rate than the repayment demands, there should be no problem.

During the 1950s, rapidly increasing aid allowed several countries to increase the deficit on their balance of trade. When aid stagnated during the 1960s, deficits diminished. The problem during that decade was not, as was stated in so many speeches and pamphlets, 'the constantly growing deficits of the developing countries', but the exact opposite. The meanness of the industrial countries over aid caused the deficits to be smaller than they ought to have been (38).

The debt burden naturally increased throughout the 1950s and 1960s when calculated at current prices, i.e. in dollars whose value increasingly diminished. But the capacity to pay interest and instalments on loans also grew. If we compare the inreasing flow of repayments with the growing exports, we find that these evolved on fairly parallel lines for most of the developing countries during 1960–73. The debt burden was a critical problem for only a few developing countries before the crisis of the seventies. Most of the largest debt burdens related to OPEC states or to developing countries with rapidly growing exports (39).

The deep recession that began in 1973 signified a dramatic change. The deficits on the trade balance of the expansive developing countries* increased rapidly. Financing was largely done on commercial terms and the repayment demands increased more rapidly than exports. Several countries are now in or on the brink of an acute crisis.

There are many good reasons for reducing debts, renegotiating repayment terms of facilitating continued deficit financing for a number of developing countries. But this applies mainly to relatively wealthy, expansive developing countries and should not be confused with aid and endeavours to achieve global equality. This is a way of getting the old capitalist order going again. With Sweden's present economic structure a solution of these problems is in our own interest — but it should not be allowed to involve measures which erode our solidarity with the poor peoples of the world.

* See p. 78.

THE FORGOTTEN AID

In recent years the traditional form of aid has fallen into the background in the Swedish debate on the developing countries. The enthusiasm that was mobilised to get parliament to establish the 1 per cent target in the 1960s is now directed towards new and more exciting matters such as trade, monetary issues, adjustment policies and shipping. These are usually assumed to be of greater importance to the developing countries.

It is therefore as well to make it quite clear that our aid is, has been, and will for a long time remain our most tangible contribution — measured in real resources (40) that we have voluntarily foregone. That more developing countries will, we hope, win an increasing share of the world's resources for themselves is a different matter.

Aid could also be an extremely essential part of an equitable world order for the poorest people in the world. Let us assume that all industrialised countries, all the Eastern bloc states and the OPEC countries which have large surpluses on current accounts agreed to give up 1 per cent of their GDP, i.e. just over the 0.7 per cent target of the UN, to the developing countries which in 1975 had an overall output per inhabitant of $300 or less. In that case those developing countries — with over a billion inhabitants — would have at their disposal an amount corresponding to 30–35 per cent of their aggregate GNP. This inflow of resources largely absorbed by production costs — and would make it theoretically possible to triple investments (41).

If one pursues this cherished dream and imagines that governments and authorities in those countries would adopt and implement basic needs strategy, then a new and equitable order would undoubtedly be possible for the poor. This would be true even if one lowers the requirements on the 'donor countries' and widens the circle of recipient countries. One condition is that the aid is granted without commercial strings attached and is combined with effective technical assistance. This is very important. It is quite clear today that a not inconsiderable part of the aid from the wealthy countries has an insignificant or even adverse effect on the recipient country (42).

The aid targets indicated above are based on several conditions that are unrealistic today. It should nevertheless be reiterated. Aid is probably the most effective method of furthering an equitable world order. It can be channelled directly to the relevant needs. It can be geared to the recipient country's own development plans. And one day perhaps the developing countries will be able to extract more aid by discriminating against the very meanest donor countries. If one looks at the real value of the aid of certain industrialised countries today, such measures would seem to be justified — even if utopian.

One demand by the developing countries which comes very close to official development assistance is the link between special drawing rights (SDR) and the transfer of resources to developing countries (43). This proposal has been discussed in many different guises ever since it was presented at the end of the 1960s. In its very simplest form the proposal means that when new SDRs are created within the IMF, the developing countries are to get a greater share than they do at present when the distribution of SDR's is based on the size of the IMF quotas. It is difficult to see any weighty objections to this. Presuming that the member countries agree that a certain amount of liquidity is required, it seems reasonable that the poorest countries, in the first place, should receive most or at least more than today. The industrialised countries will have to earn their required amount of SDR by exporting to the developing countries. The problem now is that the IMF does not control the additional amounts of liquidity. The American dollar still predominates as international currency and it is created by means of deficits in the United States' balance of current payments.

Another possible use for SDR in the future may be to adjust the additional amounts of liquidity to the business cycle. As economic activity declines, SDR would then be distributed in order to sustain international demand. In this case too, however, SDR would have to be established as a dominating international means of payment.

One objection to all the attempts to link the transfer of resources to developing countries with SDR is that it is unnecessarily complicated since traditional aid would have the same result. Why burden and possibly weaken the monetary system with something that could be done so much more simply? And if wealthy countries are unwilling to give more aid, why then should they be prepared to give away SDRs? These objections are correct but they are not as convincing as they seem. In the first place it is not at all complicated to distribute SDRs in a new way. Today SDRs are distributed according to the quotas in the IMF — it would be no problem to use another criterion for distribution. In the second place one should not forget the psychological and cosmetical aspects. Everyone knows that aid is financed out of taxes — and it is only in a few industrialised countries that cooperation with developing countries is actively supported by the electorate. But connections between creating and distributing SDRs, on the one hand, and increased taxes in a member country, on the other, is a diffuse one. It may thus be easier to provide the developing countries with increased resources by means of SDR than through increased aid.

Notes

1. Solomon, p. 5.
2. Hudson (1977), pp. 72-73; GATT (1974), p. 31.
3. An interesting discussion of the relations of developing countries to the international system is to be found in Rothstein. Note, for instance, Rothstein's argument about their interest in the world polarisation. This is an important condition for their ability to extract advantages for themselves.
4. It is interesting to compare the World Bank's treatment of the European countries that obtained loans after the war with its treatment of developing countries. The national survey of the Netherlands in 1947, for instance, is reminiscent mostly of a bad travel brochure. The Dutch are described as 'skilful and industrious' and their government 'has given proof of stability and wisdom' (Mason & Asher, p. 153). When applications for loans from the developing countries began to arrive the conditions were tightened up considerably (ibid., p. 155 et seq.).
4a. A discussion of these problems is to be found in Trilateral Commission, p. 97 et seq.
5. On this very point, however, the text was extensively amended at the Seventh Special Session of the General Assembly. A compromise was then reached by which the UN's Trade and Development Confernece (UNCTAD) is exhorted to 'assess the need for and feasibility of inviting the major aid-giving, credit-using and borrowing countries as soon as possible to a conference to . . etc'. The UN General Assembly in 1975 urges a UNCTAD conference (in which the

same delegates of the same countries participate) to consider whether a conference should possibly be convened. One wonders how this could be done
'as soon as possible'.

6.   Amuzegar.
7.   Perez-Guerrero.
8.   Dagens Nyheter, 16 September 1975.
9.   Radetzki, p. 151.
10. Tucker, p. 53.
11. Tucker, pp. 81–83. Tucker's own theory is that the wealthy countries will
     attempt to disengage their economies from those of the developing countries
     (p. 91).
12. Perez-Guerrero.
13. Bhagwati (stencil).
14. Quoted in Silk, p. 39.
15. Perez-Guerrero.
16. Quoted in Tucker, p. 75.
17. OECD (1977).
18. This theory is explained in Prebisch (1964) and Prebisch (1970).
19. Singer's explanation of the theory is to be found in Singer (1964).
20. The first of these was really a report from the League of Nations, although it
     was not published until 1945. See Hilgerdt. The figure was repeated in United
     Nations (1962).
21. Bairoch, pp. 112–123.
22. The UN Food and Agricultural Organization (FAO) has in several publications
     warned of a threatening food shortage. An account of these is given in 'Sveriges
     aamarbete med u-landerna', SOU 1977: 13, p. 81. Keith Griffin is one of those
     who are convinced that large surpluses of foodstuffs will be produced. See e.g.
     Griffin, Keith: 'The Political Economy of Agrarian Change: An Essay on the
     Green Revolution'. Harvard University Press, Cambridge, Mass., 1974. A
     lengthy discussion of future supply and demand for raw materials is to be
     found in 'Resurserna, samhallet och framtiden' (Resources, Society and the
     Future).
23. Vaitsos, p. 16; Fong & Lim, p. 11.
24. Perez-Guerrero. The numerous references to Perez-Guerrero is explained by
     the fact that he is one of the key spokesmen for the group of developing
     countries. He led the group of developing countries which participated in the
     North-South dialogue (see p. 111).
25. Bosson & Varon, p. 31 et seq.
26. It should in all honesty be said that there have been attempts – in our view
     not particularly convincing – to present Thomas Aquinas as a modern price
     theoretician. See e.g. Worland, pp. 504–521.
27. Chydenius, p. 27.
28. A very extensive plan to stabilise the prices of 30 or so primary commodities
     was elaborated by the economists Albert G. Hart, Nicholas Kaldor and Jan
     Tinbergen in preparation for the first UNCTAD conference in 1964. See
     UNCTAD (Feb. 17, 1964). This plan aimed to stabilise the prices through
     market operations by a transformed IMF which would also provide larger
     amounts of international liquidity backed by the value of accumulated com-
     modity stocks. One snag with this programme was that the developing coun-
     tries' share of the exports which were to be stabilised was only 58 per cent.
     According to fairly optimistic calculations by critical economists the costs of
     the plan would amount to almost $4 billions by 1973 and the increase in the

export revenues of the developing countries to $1.3 billions. The costs have been calculated by Grubel (1965), pp. 130–35. A discussion of the Hart–Kaldor–Tinbergen plan is presented in Johnson.

29. Haq, p. 150.
30. Some of the more or less classical studies dealing with price and revenue stabilisation are the abovementioned Hart–Kaldor–Tinbergen report and Coppock, MacBean, Erb & Schiavo-Campo, IBRD (1968), Massell (1969) and Grubel (1975). Studies made in recent years include Knudsen & Parnes, Yotopoulos & Nugent, Kreinin & Finger, Kofi, Bieri & Schmitz, Massell (1970) and Brook & Grilli. The last mentioned work is a summary of a more extensive World Bank study.
31. MacBean, p. 109.
32. Knudsen & Parnes.
33. Kreinin & Finger.
34. Nirumand.
35. Some relevant studies of the shipping field are those by Fasbender & Wagner, Heaver and Deakin.
36. Yeats (Reprint Series No. 87).
37. An analysis of the problems of the Swedish shipping industry is presented in Wijkman.
38. Sveriges samarbete med u-landerna. SOU 1977: 13, pp. 100–102.
39. Ask.
40. There are many strange notions in the debate about the 'cost' of aid. It should thus be made clear that the cost is exactly the sum allocated in the budget. It is a measure of the real resources that we refrain from using ourselves. That the balance of payments effect is considerably less is quite another matter. Tying of aid which gives rise to subsidies to Swedish enterprises can reduce the cost, but that effect is still marginal.
41. Calculations based on UNCTAD (1977), Table 1.3, 6.1.A and 6.1.B.
42. Mende, pp. 181–83; Byres, p. 47 et seq.; Brecher & Abbas, p. 32; Anell (1978). Some decision-makers in wealthy countries entertain the remarkable notion that all commodities and products they have in surplus – dried fish or prefabricated wooden houses, foodstuffs or simple manual tools – will necessarily promote development in the developing countries. In criticising aid one must remember that a very considerable part of it has never had a developmental effect as its primary purpose. The motive has instead been one of strategic, commercial or cultural policy.
43. A discussion of the SDR link is to be found in Bhagwati (1977), pp. 81–104.

5. AN EQUITABLE WORLD ORDER

It is natural that the debate about changed relationships between rich and poor countries should proceed from the demands presented by the developing countries. But it would appear to be a mistake to start with the assumption — which is often made in Sweden — that the proposals are both correct and morally justified *simply* because they have been formulated by the developing countries.

Generally speaking the moral right of the developing countries to make demands on the rich countries is very rarely questioned. But in what does this moral right consist? There are several possible answers to that question. Some may regard the present aid as a repayment of the colonial debt of the Western world. Others regard development aid as a marginal contribution to compensate for the injustices in the existing world order.*

The basic motive for aid, however, is the enormous differences in income — if the developing countries were not so much poorer there would never by any question of even discussing long-term aid or other forms of support. This is also roughly the answer chosen by the Pearsson Commission. 'The simplest answer to the question is the moral one: that it is only right for those who have to share with those who have not' (1).

The moral right of the developing countries is thus based on the fact that they are so much poorer than the industrialised countries. Consequently the poorer a country is the greater is its

* There are also many who believe that aid can be justified as support for development towards a more peaceful world. This is doubtful, however, It seems more likely that development and rapid changes lead to increased instability and new tensions. There are many reasons for aid but we should hardly expect to get a more peaceful world 'into the bargain'.

moral right to make demand. But the moral question obviously does not relate to the differences in incomes between countries; it relates to the enormous gap in resources between the poor people in developing countries and the relatively wealthy majority of the population in the industrialised countries. To be more precise, then: the governments of the developing countries seem to have a moral right to demand aid and changes in the existing international economic order because it is assumed that these measures — at least in the long run — will benefit the poor people in the developing countries. Or to state the salient points: if the right of the developing countries to make demands is based on the differences in income between poor and rich prople in the world, then it follows that they can *only* demand measures which — at least in the long run — will lead to a transfer of income between these two groups, i.e. from rich people in both industrialised and developing countries to poor people in the developing countries.

These questions very rarely come up in the debate on developing countries. It is presumably regarded as unfitting even to discuss the moral right of the governments of developing countries to make demands on the rich countries.

But is it so obvious? What right has the government of a developing country to demand increased taxation of the citizens in the industrialised countries if they themselves do not even try to tax their own upper class — but instead, as happens in several developing countries, use aid and other state revenues to directly favour an already wealthy elite? It is easy to understand the desire of the developing countries to be able to sell more manufactured goods in the markets of the industrialised countries. This is where the purchasing power exists. But surely this demand should be supplemented by efforts to widen the domestic market, i.e. apply distributive policies that will also enable the citizens of their own country to buy the consumer goods in question. From the point of view of actual needs it is in the populous developing countries that the major markets exist for clothing, food, health services and housing.

Does not the moral motive for giving aid in fact presuppose that the governments of both industrialised and developing countries actively participate in a concerted effort for a more equitable international distribution of resources? And should not measures be carried out in such a way that they reach the poor people if they are to be justifiable on moral grounds? These are some of the questions we shall deal with below.

INTERNATIONAL AND NATIONAL PROBLEMS

The UN resolution on NIEO deals only with inter-state relations. That is no coincidence. The leading spokesmen for developing countries have in recent years made it clear that international conferences should only make recommendations about inter-state relations, while each sovereign state will decide its own internal affairs. It is easy to understand and respect this stance. All countries want to decide their own affairs without external pressures. And the developing countries must regard it as particularly important to defend their, often newly-won, political independence. The leaders of many developing countries have known the degradation of colonialism, and neo-colonialism is not, in fact, simply a Marxist invention.

In this connection it is instructive to compare the strong and unanimous support of the developing countries for NIEO with their attitude to the basic needs strategy adopted at the World Employment Conference of the International Labour Organisation (ILO) in the summer of 1976 (2). This strategy is a recommendation to all countries, in practice primarily developing countries, to direct their development policies towards satisfying the poorest people's needs of food, clothing, dwellings, health services, drinking water, education, and the power to influence their own situation. At the above-mentioned conference, which was formally a technical committee subordinate to the board of the ILO, a declaration was unanimously adopted that underlined the need for urgent measures to attack the problems of the poor population groups. When the question was dealt with later in the summer by the UN's Economic and Social Council (ECOSOC) the developing countries were doubtful about the proposals from the ILO conference. No decision could be reached to pass the question on to the UN General Assembly. The declaration on a basic needs strategy therefore has not the same international status as the NIEO recommendations. In subsequent years the governments of the developing countries have become more openly sceptical towards the basic needs strategy.

The reason why the developing countries are doubtful about the 'basic needs philosophy' is simple and not wholly unjustified They see it as an attempt on the part of the rich countries to meddle in their internal affairs. The developing countries have therefore indicated their position in roughly the following way. First, the industrialised countries must agree to introduce a new world order. The increased resources which this will give the developing countries will be available for use in fulfilling the poorest people's needs for the barest necessities.

There is no doubt, however, that certain developing countries are anxious to distract attention from the internal problems of distribution. In that situation NIEO may be regarded as a good excuse. Measures of international support are presented as a necessary precondition for tackling domestic problems. It is therefore logical to try to focus the international negotiations on the rules of the game for cooperation between the nations of the world. Only after that will it become relevant and feasible to pursue a national policy of redistribution.

This attitude rests on a weak empirical basis. The authors of the ILO report on the basic needs strategy come to virtually the opposite conclusion. Measures taken in the sphere of trade, for instance, are 'unlikely to have a significant and immediate impact on mass poverty and inequality' (3). National measures are quite decisive if one wants to improve the situation for the poor (3). Several governments of developing countries have also shown that even with the existing world order it is possible to pursue an effective redistribution policy (4).

Every country naturally has the right to assert its sovereignty and independence. It is only when the developing countries *at the same time* demand a new international economic order and stand up for their complete sovereignty that new problems arise.

We can here ignore the fact that the demands of the developing countries affect the internal affairs of the industrialised countries. The important question is whether NIEO will contribute to increased global equity. Is it enough that resources are transferred from one group of countries to another? Does the front line in the struggle for equity really run along national frontiers? Has capital suddenly become patriotic? Is it no longer the case that equity and distribution are primarily a question of who own and control?

Let us look at how NIEO relates to and interacts with the national orders in the developing countries. What would happen if one succeeded in transferring resources to developing countries through a new international economic order?

The simple — and quite correct — answer to that question is that the increasing resources will be distributed according to the inequitable pattern which is described on pp. 63-70. Only in a few developing countries will the broad masses of the people receive a share in the growing resources (5).

That is hardly an optimistic conclusion which is close to the thoughts of Robert W. Tucker: 'The state is at once the principal instrument through which a hoped-for redistribution is to be effected and the principal obstacle in the way of such redistribution' (6).

Our own thesis goes something like this. The government of a developing country that wants to implement a policy of justice faces very great problems, far greater than any government of an industrialised country has been able to tackle — with the exception of Japan which succeeded with a virtually confiscatory land reform. It is thus not always sufficient to try to redistribute the annual increase of resources, as was done in Europe during the later phases of industrialisation. Nor is a relatively smooth distribution of resources an automatic consequence of the development process in developing countries, as was partly the case in the European countries during their industrialisation. It is often necessary for the developing countries to attempt to redistribute existing wealth, above all arable land. It goes without saying that a firm populat basis is a necessary precondition for the success of a distributive policy of that kind.

At the same time it is perfectly clear that the decisive measures of distributive policy in the world of today must be taken by governments and authorities in the developing countries.

The necessary measures can be facilitated through international support. But it is not possible to maintain that NIEO is a necessary precondition for a distributive policy in the developing countries. It is quite simply an illusion to believe that the decisive questions of equity in the world are solved at international negotiating tables. It is still the case that the overwhelming number of decisions that directly affect people's situation are taken within national states.

And if we look closer at the proposals from the UN, it becomes clear that many of them require open or hidden decisions on distributive policy by governments in the recipient countries. Let us, for example, look at how a commodity agreement with export quotas functions. In order to succeed in raising prices all the participating countries must limit their exports to the agreed quota. If prices are raised, it will obviously be very important for the individual producers in the country to get as large a slice of the national allocation as possible. The government must then decide who are to benefit and who are to be left out (7). Will the large plantation owners share the quota or will the multitude of peasants be given a chance to increase their cash incomes? Which groups control the decisions?

Practically every transfer of resources which is put at the direct disposal of a government requires that a decision is taken on distribution. Most of the developing countries have adopted measures which strictly limit imports. This means that many imports command a very high price — often far higher than the current price on the world market.

Let us now assume that a government receives an aid delivery of artificial fertiliser as a gift. The government can then either sell it at the high market price — and use the proceeds for normal state expenditure — or set the price lower and give a subsidy to the purchasers. But who should be allowed to purchase — the big landowners or the peasants? And which enterprise is to benefit from the foreign consultant? Who should be licensed to import necessary spare parts?

The governments in developing countries are constantly forced to make decisions which will determine the distribution of resources in the country. And these decisions are in many cases almost totally unrelated to whether we have a new or an old world order; they depend exclusively on the policy that the government is pursuing.

Hitherto the poorest groups of people in many, if not the majority of, developing countries have been left out of the development that is taking place (8). Aid has largely been directed towards the modern sector and on projects which are profitable in the short term. Technology has been concentrated in export industries. The traditional elites have privately appropriated the profits but have socialised the losses in the commodity trade (9).

There is no point in discussing global equality in terms of gulfs and confrontation between countries. The wide and rapidly growing gap runs between the poorest billion of the earth's inhabitants, who have not received very much of the rapid increase in resources during the last 20–25 years, and the rest of the earth's population in industrialised countries, developing countries and Eastern bloc countries. That is the problem. And it can only be solved if an equitable international economic order is linked to equitable national orders.

The question is now whether international agreements can be formulated in such a way that they directly benefit the poorest people. The most reasonable solution would be, for example, that commodity agreements on higher prices simultaneously provided higher wages and better working conditions for those who mine the ore and cultivate the soil.

The International Metal Workers' Federation has put forward the idea of a 'social clause' in connection with the trade negotiations in GATT. The purpose is that all countries that participate in international trade should be forced to guarantee certain basic social conditions for the workers. The idea is not as revolutionary as it may seem. The International Labour Organisation (ILO) has adopted numerous recommendations over the years relating to trade union work and conditions of employment. But these resolutions have no bite because they are not linked to any sanctions. And that is what's new in the proposal for a social clause. Only countries that guarantee reasonable conditions for the workers would be entitled to tariff reductions in accordance with the most-favoured-nation principle or to preferences.

It is obvious that the proposal could be extended to other fields. Why should developing countries that make a good living by functioning as tax havens and addresses for mail-box companies be given special trading privileges (10)? Some industrialised countries try to punish serious violations of elementary human rights by cancelling or reducing aid. But may not sanctions in the sphere of trade be more effective?

It will never be feasible to demand that European working conditions are applied by the developing countries. What one may envisage are, for example, demands for a minimum wage at a reasonable level, limitation of working hours to, say 10 hours a day, certain trade union rights and a ban on child labour. That alone, however, would according to some critics have negative effects in the developing countries. Above all, improved working conditions would raise production costs and lead to unemployment. And a bad job is better than none at all.

But is it certain that reasonable minimum conditions for the workers would have that effect? In several of the rapidly industrialising developing countries the productivity of labour is as high as in Europe and the United States, but wages are only one tenth. In South Korea teenage girls work to accumulate dowries by spending 11 hours a day, six days a week, sewing suits which are exported for about 25 dollars and are sold by Hennes & Mauritz, a low-price clothing chain in Stockholm, for about 100 dollars. These differences in prices and wages ought, in all reason, to make it possible to spare South Korean women working in the textile industry the necessity of having to live in barracks for three years of their lives, without competitive power being lost.

Conditions in Singapore are instructive in another way. In only three years, 1968-71, this state became, second only to Japan, Asia's leading manufacturer of semiconductors for the electronics industry. Despite the great turnover in manpower several American enterprises regard manpower productivity of labour there as higher than in the United States. The Singapore government thought that the workers should receive a share of the growth and therefore ordered a substantial wage increase and certain other improvements during 1973–74. The transnational corporations immediately began to look around for countries with cheaper labour. And in the electronics industry, for example, they are not tied down by large fixed investments. The enterprises usually have little capital of their own in relation to turnover and the investment per employee amounted to about $4500 in the mid-70s (11).

In the absence of international minimum employment standards the developing countries may thus be forced, against their will, to undercut each other by offering their workers wages and wretched working conditions.

It is not certain that the threat of transnationals moving out is always serious, however. It seems clear that above all they are searching for stable, predictable environments and expanding markets. Tax concessions and low wages have hitherto played a relatively small part, even if the importance of labour costs is increasing. There it should be possible for the governments that wish to attract transnational corporations to combine such a policy with tolerable working conditions. And higher wages mean not only increased production costs but also increased consumer demand.

There is — and this should not be forgotten — a moral issue involved here. A social clause would be generally applicable — and thus quite compatible with free trade principles — but in practice would hit the developing countries. And those insisting on it would be the rich countries that once imposed an extreme free trade regime on developing countries without worrying about the conditions of the workers.

There is also in some quarters a hope that a social clause would restrict exports from the newly industrialising countries. It is hardly likely, however, that such an effect would be more than marginal. A social clause of reasonable scope is unlikely to affect the competitive edge of those countries very much. A growing domestic market can absorb part of the output, but the purchasing power will still be in the rich countries.

In our opinion, the social clause is worth serious consideration. If it can be made operative we should for the first time have a world order which not only provides freedom for enterprises, goods and capital — but also provides advantages to those who produce the goods.

Another important point: is there a realistic alternative to

the social clause? Will governments and trade unions in the rich
countries accept competition which they consider has its roots
in unacceptable working conditions? In all events wretched
conditions for workers in developing countries will give a
'moral' boost to the already strong demands for increased
protectionism. If the social clause can contribute to traditional
arguments about efficiency. A rapid development towards
protectionism and regulation of trade will give rise to effects
that are difficult to forecast and therefore involve a waste of
the real resources that have been invested in anticipation of a
continued 'normal' development. It is quite possible that an
agreement on a social clause, even for the NIC countries, is the
second best but only conceivable solution, on condition that
the industrialised countries are prepared to guarantee reasonable freedom of trade.

NEW OR EQUITABLE INTERNATIONAL ECONOMIC ORDER

Only during the 1970s have the differences between rich and
poor developing countries been given serious attention in international negotiations. As recently as at the second UN Conference on Trade and Development (UNCTAD II) in 1968 this
question hardly came up in the debate. Now there are several
international resolutions pointing to the special needs of the
poorest developing countries. It is only in connection with
official development assistance, however, that any measures
have been taken — and not even in this sphere are the poorest
countries given any priority in the distribution of existing
resources. The 1977 annual report of the chairman of OECD's
Development Assistance Commiteee states that 39 non-oil
exporting developing countries, with an aggregate population
of 1200 million and an average per capita GDP of less than
$150, received only half as much aid per inhabitant throughout
the 1970s as other, wealthier developing countries. This figure
is, however, heavily influenced by India, which gets extremely
little aid per inhabitant. If one looks only at the remaining 38
countries, they do get about the same amount per capita as

the wealthier developing countries. Furthermore a clear increase in aid to the 29 least advanced developing countries is noted in the report (12). Yet the wealthier developing countries are still favoured even in the sphere of aid — however this is calculated.

The texts from the Sixth Special Session of the General Assembly also contain a few passages about the particular needs of the poorest developing countries. But it is quite obvious that the measures which the industrialised countries are urged to adopt in the UN resolution, are designed to give formally equal benefits to all developing countries, irrespective of their economic situations or the aims of their distribution of resources policies.

We must therefore ask ourselves what effects NIEO may have on the distribution of power and resources between various countries. In the next section we shall deal with the advantages that developing countries can secure for themselves without the approval of the industrialised countries.

The central proposals in the UN resolution are to apply equally to all — roughly like the old GATT rules. But that does not mean that all benefit to the same degree. Export gains will mainly accrue to those developing countries which are able to increase their exports at competitive prices. All studies so far show that it is a very small group of the more advanced developing countries that has really gained from tariff preferences (13), which in themselves offer quite small overall benefits. And these countries would also be favoured most of all by a general liberalisation of world trade (14). The transfer of technology will never be free of charge even if the terms governing it are made easier. Above all, the recipient country must be able to assimilate and adapt the transferred technology. There is no doubt that it is the developing countries which are best equipped industrially that benefit from the NIEO proposals in the technology field (15). Borrowing facilities on the capital markets of the industrialised countries is another essential. This would primarily be of advantages to the wealthier and more creditworthy developing countries. The proposals on commodities are more difficult to assess, but it seems most likely that they will primarily benefit countries which already have the advantage of exporting the more attractive commodities, which can command higher prices and are protected against substitutes. Apart from the Special Programme for the developing countries that were most seriously affected by the crisis, which was never very extensive and has now come to an end, it is actually difficult to see any proposals in the UN resolution which would be of particular benefit to the least developed countries. This may also be true of proposals for increased food aid.

It is difficult to be certain about the effects that the New International Economic Order will have, as proposals are rather vague. The qualified conjecture that we share with the majority of other observers — most of whom are considerably surer of themselves — is: the New International Economic Order will in the long term result in a transfer of resources from industrialised to developing countries. The countries within the latter group which will benefit most are those that already have a relatively well developed industrial capacity, can even today borrow on the international capital market, are even now effective competitors of the enterprises of the industrialised countries, and have long since achieved a rapid growth of GNP and export revenues. It is therefore probable that the ones that will benefit from the new order are primarily those countries which are doing fairly well under the old.

This situation, together with the realisation that the developing countries do not really demand a new world order but only rather modest reforms of the old one, has given rise to some rather cynical speculations. Tom I. Fahrer, for example, maintains that the United States only needs to win over the ruling elites in a few states — Nigeria, Brazil, Venezuela, Mexico, India and Indonesia — in order to retain the old order. The strategy aims to split the group of developing countries, by winning over the more conservative ones and isolating the radical (16). Sometimes this idea is elaborated to imply that the poorest countries are of no significance and must therefore get along as best they can. This would be a parallel to the process which has taken place in many countries — new elites push to the fore and are given a share of the privileges of power in the hope that they will forget their old allies on the barricades. Johan Galtung is one of those who regard this as one of the likely alternatives.

But what if we are serious about global equity? How should the international system of rules be designed so that it directs the flow of resources to the poorer developing countries? The answer is simple. The measures adopted in all fields should discriminate in favour of the countries that are worst off, at least as long as this can be done without causing efficiency losses in the system as a whole.

In hundreds of resolutions from international conferences the rich countries are urged to adopt a whole series of measures to benefit the developing countries (18). In order to enjoy these benefits — when and if they come into effect — it is enough to be defined as a developing country. This, by the way, is one of the most important reasons for the relatively rich developing countries to try to keep the whole group of developing countries together. Without this division of the whole world into *two* groups — one that is to give and one that is to receive — several fairly wealthy and reactionary developing countries would not be morally and politically able to demand privileged treatment from the rich, industrialised countries.

Let us take the most obvious cases first. There is no reason whatsoever to give financial aid to wealthy OPEC states. Nor should other assistance or concessions be required, as these countries can so obviously pay to satisfy their needs. Apart from the OPEC states there are several other developing countries that achieved a rapid economic growth and thereby at least the chance to look after the needs of their citizens more effectively. But in the majority of poor developing countries the growth of productive capacity only just keeps pace with the increase in population. This development, which implies a rapidly widening gulf between richer and poorer developing countries, has been proceeding throughout the postwar period.

Looked at as a simplified problem of equity it seems reasonable to think in terms of a division into three groups (such as is largely the case *within* the welfare states), namely one group that receives (the poor developing countries), one that gives (the rich, industrialised countries and some OPEC states) and a middle group that neither receives nor gives. One problem with this 'solution' is, of course, that this is a classification of countries according to *average income*. Really poor people exist in all three groups. But the average GDP and its rate of growth does, when all is said and done, provide a rough gauge of the economic potential of a government to handle the situation, if it has the political will to do so.

It is often maintained that certain measures, such as preferences, revenue stabilisation and favourable terms for the transfer of technology must be applied generally. This is quite wrong. To introduce tariff preferences, i.e. particularly advantageous rules for products from a certain country or countries, is one thing. Which countries should receive preferences is quite another question (19). Tariff preferences were introduced in order to give the developing countries a competitive advantage over the industrialised countries in the international market. The developing countries were not regarded as capable of competing on equal terms as the old GATT rules presupposed. It certainly sounds generous to say that the preferences are to apply equally to all developing countries. But should Afghanistan have to complete on equal terms with Mexico? Does Rwanda not need more support than South Korea? Is it not more reasonable here as well as to have at least three groups, one that receives and one that grants preferences, and a third that has a uniform same-for-all tariff.

When it comes to measures to stabilise the price of a commodity every important producer should, in all reason, be involved. But a programme to stabilise export revenues does not have to include all developing countries. It is quite possible to limit participation to the poorest countries. It should similarly be possible to grant improved access to technology on favourable terms to countries which have no chance of acquiring it by commercial means.

There are thus abundant means of discriminating within a planned new international economic order in favour of the poorer developing countries. As we have already said, whether this is politically feasible remains, as we said above, an open question.

It is easy, however, to justify an orientation of the world order towards the poor countries. The sum of the concessions that the industrialised countries can make — whether these take the form of assistance and SDRs, of lowering tariffs, of accepting higher commodity prices or of promoting the transfer of technology — is limited. Those who have the greatest needs — and the best motives — should get the major share. And several developing countries get along very well, as we have said, under the 'old' economic order.

UNITY AND NEGOTIATING STRENGTH

Negotiations to change the international economic order have been going on since the fifties. When UNCTAD was set up the activity increased noticeably and at present 3–5 world conferences and hundreds of other intergovernmental meetings take place every year. The result of this activity — the costs of which run into many tens of millions of dollars — is conspicuously meagre and one wonders why the developing countries continue to negotiate.

The industrialised countries will not surrender their privileges as long as there is any chance of keeping them. A protracted negotiating process that results in non-committal recommendations is actually an excellent way for the rich countries to gain time. And yet the developing countries try to reach a settlement at the negotiation table. Why?

There are several simple and partially correct answers to this question. The financial costs are very small for the developing countries. So even if it is only possible to achieve marginal changes it may be worth the effort. There is an extensive international bureaucracy with a strong self-interest in all negotiations. The international organisations are designed for negotiations. Proposals that are put forward thus lead to negotiations, studies by secretariats, working parties, meetings of experts and conferences. And the conferences are both stimulating and profitable for the delegates. There is simply the growth of the international negotiating machinery — apart from the politically motivated calls to economise from some major powers.

But there are other and more significant explanations of why the developing countries stake such a large part of their resources at the world's negotiating table. A negotiating routine has developed which really only favours the rich countries. All new problems are put on the international agenda along with the old ones. The international agencies are always looking for new tasks — often resulting in duplication and time-consuming so-called coordination.

It is taken as such a matter of course that one should negotiate with the industrialised countries on all international problems and the developing countries seldom think about possible alternatives. And what is more, the developing countries have largely defined their problems as being caused by the rich countries. Yet the most natural thing to do would be for the group of developing countries, or smaller groups of them, *first* to consider whether they could not take measures of their own to *force* the industrialised countries to accept various changes.

The problem is, however, that most developing countries have inadequate resources to investigate problems and insufficient information about the rest of the world. For example, when the countries in West Africa negotiated with the EEC in the 1960s, they had to rely on foreign, primarily French, experts (20). The UNCTAD secretariat does to some extent function as the research organisation of the developing countries and, as such, makes a very valuable contribution. But an international organisation can never take the place of what the developing countries need more than anything — an organisation of their own to mobilise the collective power necessary to enforce a change of the world order. Today the developing countries are formally at least united on a large number of questions. But this unity gives little strength. The demands of the developing countries must be backed by the threat of alternative measures. And it is precisely in order to work out this strategy that the developing countries need their own organisation — if they intend to continue fighting together.

It is not up to us to prescribe what a strategy for the developing countries should or could be, but we can anyway mention a few possibilities.

The most obvious one is aid. Why do the developing countries not force the industrialised countries to increase the flow of aid and raise its quality? As commercial motives play a significant part in shaping the aid policies of several countries the threat of trade discrimination ought to be an effective method. It is practiced to varying degrees by the regional banks. These do not permit purchase to be made in countries that make no contributions. If the majority of developing countries could stick together, it would suffice if they jointly declared that they intended to think twice before inviting tenders from enterprises in the two or three industrialised countries which supply least aid. In that way they would induce the competition which the 0.7 per cent target was intended to stimulate.

Why have the developing countries been negotiating so long about codes of conduct for the transfer of technology and about transnational corporations? The governments of industrialised countries will not voluntarily agree to anything but pretty meaningless recommendations. And even if one regards international calls for honesty and sound business principles as useful, it is still the individual developing country's access to information that is decisive. Such a simple thing as an organised cooperation to establish a list of honest consultancy firms and a file of information on technology procurement would be of great value to several developing countries. This cannot be done by a UN agency because of the supposed objectivity it would have to observe. A developing country organisation, on the other hand, could without hesitation blacklist a consulting firm which had been guilty of misconduct — and this would be an effective threat. The recently established Information Centre of the non-aligned states in Havana appears to be an embryo of the type of organisation that is required.

Why do so many developing countries accept the rich countries' legislation on patents and copyright — not to speak of the transnational corporations rights to their trademarks? Should not centuries of colonialism and exploitation render it both justified and excusable if the developing countries simply stole the patents of the big corporations and made use of copyrights without compensation? It is not as easy as it sounds, but it has been done — the Japanese made use of patented knowledge without paying for it and it has not been long since the Soviet Union translated books without paying any compensation.

The weak position of the developing countries with regard to industrial technology is more pronounced than in almost any other sphere. And this information gulf is of an extremely crucial significance. Developing countries' control over scientific and technical resources — patented or not — decides how effectively they can exploit resources in other spheres and determines their position in negotiations with transnational corporations among others.

Today the developing countries together hold only 1 per cent of the total patent rights in the world (21) and it is a small group of countries that accounts for the majority of that percentage. Many transnational corporations have registered their patents in developing countries without making use of them there. The purpose is merely to prevent competition (22). Studies of the situation in Latin American countries indicate that an increasing share of patent rights are held by foreigners (22). In one UNCTAD study the patent system that is based on the Paris Convention of 1883 is characterised as a 'reverse system of preferences to the benefit of foreign patent holders' (23).

In the expansive markets patents probably play a diminishing role. An extensive technological and organisational infrastructure is required to establish effective production even if one possesses the formal right. Patents do still have a role to play, however, 'as a subsidiary device for supporting strongly oligopolistic market structures' (24).

Several researchers, among them Sanjaya Lall and Edith Penrose, maintain that those developing countries which have chosen a capitalist development model probably benefit from accepting the international patent rules (25). Some developing countries have nevertheless decided to forego this 'profit'. In Brazil, patent protection for drugs was abolished in 1972; in Mexico in 1976. India provides such short-term patent protection that is in practice of no value for the pharmaceutical companies. There are certainly reasons to investigate the possibilities of collective action on a larger scale by the developing countries in this sphere.

It is thanks to their trademarks that the big food and soft drink enterprises can dominate the market in the developing countries. And it is not just a matter of conspicuous consumption and cultural patterns among the wealthy elites. Many have testified the situation in the big slum areas in the third world where people can freely choose between seven kinds of soft drinks but lack pure drinking water.

Several developing countries have tried to produce protein-enriched soft drinks, but have been beaten in competition on equal terms with the more glamorous drinks of the transnational corporations. In Brazil, one of the world's largest orange producers, people drink Fanta, which is a completely synthetic product without any vitamin C. Previously the Coca Cola company, which manufactures Fanta, was granted tax concessions which hampered domestic competitors (26).

It is also thanks to trademarks and status advertising that Nestle and other transnational food corporations have persuaded women in developing countries to stop breast-feeding their children and instead give them a substitute for mother's milk. In areas without pure drinking water this is a direct threat to the children's lives, as the milk powder has to be mixed with water. In addition, women lose their natural protection against new pregnancies (27).

There are certainly good reasons — economic, social, medical and cultural — for the developing countries to consider banning trademark advertising and certain transnational corporations.

One idea that has been discussed from time to time is that developing countries should unilaterally decide to suspend the payment of interest and instalments on commercial loans. David O. Beim argues quite convincingly that this is not a viable strategy for individual developing countries (28). Perhaps the situation would be different if it was a concerted action by many developing countries?

Shipping companies that are jointly owned by several neighbouring developing countries is also an idea worth testing (29). UNCTAD has shown in one study that cooperation on the import side between developing countries can give large-scale economies (30). Sri Lanka has shown that it is possible to lower import costs by a state monopoly on imports of drugs.

The Andean Pact in Latin America turned out to be a short-

lived experiment. It did, however, show that control of transnational corporations can and must take place in the host
countries. By means of a careful scrutiny of the accounts of
the enterprises and their general business methods the participating countries were able to strengthen their negotiating
position considerably. The Comite de Regalias in Colombia has
saved several millions of dollars for the state treasury during its
operations (31).

In the sphere of exports the developing countries have primarily attempted to obtain better and more stable export prices.
But the big profits are made at the processing stage and in the
wholesale and retail trade. Rene Servoise has estimated that 'of
the $200 billion (not counting tax) the consumers at the end
of the line pay for primary commodities (excluding oil) imported from third world countries, the biggest cut goes to
industrial and commercial middlemen, the vast majority of
them from developed nations, while only $20 billion reaches
the producer countries'. A large part of the profit consists
of the difference between what the buyers of minerals pay to
the developing countries and what they receive from sales in the
industrialised countries (32). The commodity strategy of the
developing countries should thus aim at capturing the international trade and distribution. This would not only produce
increased revenues; it would also make it possible to circumvent
the effective tariff protection for the processing industries* of
the industrialised countries.

One objection could, of course, be that these proposals presuppose a homogeneity, unity and organisational capacity that
the group of developing countries does not possess. That may
be so. But in that case the unity at international negotiating
tables is not worth much either.

It may anyway be questioned whether the developing countries should always be united. It has always been taken for
granted that the unity which was created in the 1960s and was
later raised to a dogma does provide strength. Perez-Guerrero
says that 'the third world bases its strength on the unity between
all developing countries however big the differences may be
with regard to stage of development, access to natural resources

* See p. 60 et seq.

or other factors' (33) and this unity is based on a feeling of
solidarity which can be directly compared with that of the
trade unions after the industrial revolution in the rich countries (33). But that is not an analysis — only a doubtful parallel.
The trade unions were founded on a genuine common interest
and a united front against those who owned and controlled the
capital. This natural cohesive force exists neither between nor
within the developing countries of today. It seems not im-
probable that groups of developing countries with clear
common national interests can advance further than the group
as a whole. This is surely one of the things which OPEC demonstrated by quadrupling oil prices — a demand that the whole
group of developing countries could hardly have supported had
it been put forward in international negotiations. It should anyway be possible for actions of this kind to be launched while
at the same time maintaining the unity of the group of developing countries at international conferences, which could then,
we hope, be focussed on the questions that affect the poor
people in the world.

This is not primarily a question of development towards a
more equitable world order; it will be the stronger, more expansive developing countries that will secure greater resources for
themselves. But it is a development that will take place whether
we like it or not. And maybe we do want it. Today many of the
wealthier developing countries are harsh dictatorships. Rapid
changes set in motion forces which, with the support of the
international community, can induce hopes of a process leading
to greater democracy.

Notes

1.   Partners in Development, p. 8.
2.   ILO (1976). A description of the basic needs strategy is given on pp. 32–33.
3.   ILO (1976), p. 103.
4.   Anell (1977).
5.   Galtung believes that the situation is really even worse than that. Resources
    coming from outside always fall into the hands of the ruling elite which can
    enrich itself with them and strengthen its position of power. It is much more
    difficult to appropriate the surplus produced by independent peasants (Gal-
    tung).

6.   Tucker, p. 137.
7.   Griffin (1970).
8.   Anell (1977).
9.   Gordon, p. 375; Arraes, p. 38.
10.   Sweden and other countries today give special trading privileges (preferences),
      e.g. to the Bahamas and the Cayman Islands. One wonders if there is any
      reason for this except that they happen to belong to the group defined by the
      Statistical Office of the UN as developing countries.
11.   Fong & Lim.
12.   OECD (1977), chap. III; Campbell & Mytelka. Bhagwati (MIT Press 1977)
      demonstrates a fairly rapidly increasing share of aid to the poorer countries in
      recent years (p. 40 et seq.). See also White, p. 39 et seq., on factors determin-
      ing the extent of aid for various recipient countries.
13.   Morton & Tulloch, ch. 5; Behram.
14.   Kreinin & Finger.
15.   Teece (1977), pp. 242–61 and Teece (1976), p. 99.
16.   Fahrer.
17.   Galtung.
18.   The East European states usually play a very passive role at UN conferences
      on development questions. Their reason is that they lack 'colonial guilt' for
      the situation of the developing countries.
19.   Norway gives preferences to all developing countries, but its tariff rates for the
      very poorest countries are particularly favourable.
20.   Rothstein (1977), pp. 46–47.
21.   Ewing.
22.   Vaitsos, pp. 76–79; Ledagar, p. 63.
23.   UNCTAD (July 1975); See also Lall.
24.   Lall.
25.   Lall; Penrose. See also Grubel (1977).
26.   Ledogar, pp. 116–117. Ledogar provides a good description of the difficulties
      involved in competing with the established trademarks in the food market.
27.   The Baby Killer.
28.   Beim.
29.   Yeats (Reprint Series No. 94).
30.   UNCTAD (1975).
31.   Vaitsos, pp. 128–131.
32.   Servoise, quoted in Hudson (1977), p. 139.
33.   Perez-Guerrero.

BIBLIOGRAPHY

Adam, Gyorgy, Multinational Corporations and Worldwide sourcing in Radice, Hugo (1975).

Aktuellt i Handelspolitiken (News in Trade Policy).

Aktstycken utgivna av utrikesdepartementet, Ny serie (Documents published by the Ministry for Foreign Affairs, New Series)

    I:A:24 Forenta Nationernas generalforsamlings sjatte extra mote 9 april–2 maj 1974 (Sixth Special Session of the UN General Assembly 9 April–2 May 1974)

    I:A:25 Forenta Nationernas generalforsamlings tjugonionde ordinarie mote 1974 (the Twenty-ninth Session of the UN General Assembly 1974)

    I:A:26 Forenta Nationernas generalforsamlings sjunde extra mote 1–16 september 1975 (the Seventh Special Session of the UN General Assembly 1–16 September 1975)

    II:27 Forenta Nationernas befolkningskonferens i Bukarest 19–30 augusti 1974 (the World Population Conference in Bucharest 19–30 August 1974)

    II:28 Forenta Nationernas livsmedelskonferens i Rom 5–16 november 1974 (the World Food Conference in Rome 5–16 November 1974).

Amuzegar, Jahangir, A Requiem for the North–South Conference, Foreign Affairs, Vol 56, No 1, October 1977.

Anell, Lars, Resursfordelning och bistandsplanering. Bilaga 5 till Sveriges samarbete med u-landerna. Bilagor. SOU 1977: 14. (Distribution of Resources and Development Aid Planning. Appendix 5 to Sweden's cooperation with developing countries. Appendices.)

———— Resource Distribution and Aid Planning. EADI Seminar. Milan September 1978. (Stencil.)

Ansprenger, Franz, Kolonialvaldenas upplosning. Aldus/Bonniers. Stockholm 1968. (The Disintegration of the Colonial Empires.)

175

Arraes, Miguel, Brazil: The People and the Power. Penguin Books 1972.

Ashworth, William, Varldens affarer. Ekonomisk historia 1850-1960. Aldus. Lund 1966. (A Short History of the International Economy since 1850.)

Ask, Sten, U-landernas skuldborda. Bilaga 7 till Sveriges smarbete med u-landerna, SOU 1977: 14. (The Debt Burden of the Developing Countries. Appendix 7 to Sweden's Cooperation with Developing Countries.)

The Baby Killer. Printed by War on Want, 467 Caledonian Road, London N7 9BE. 2nd edition with appendix.

Bairoch, Paul, The Economic Development in the Third World Since 1900. University of California Press. Berkeley and Los Angeles 1975.

Barnet, Richard J. & Mueller, Ronald E., Global Reach. The Power of the Multinational Corporations. Simon and Schuster. New York 1974.

Barraclough, Geoffrey, An Introduction to Contemporary History. C. A. Watt & Co Ltd. London 1964.

———— Waiting for the New Order. New York Review of Books, October 26, 1978, pp. 45-53.

———— The Struggle for the Third World. New York Review of Books, November 9, 1978, pp. 47-58.

Behnam, M. Resa, Development and Structure of the Generalized System of Preferences. Journal of World Trade Law, Vol 9, No 6, 1975.

Beim, David O., Rescuing the LDCs. Foreign Affairs, Vol 55, No 4, July 1977.

Bhagwati, Jagdish, North-South Relations. (Stecil.) The International Economic Conference in Search of New Prosperity. Tokyo, October 26-28, 1977.

———— (ed), The New International Economic Order: The North-South Debate. The MIT Press. Cambridge, Mass. and London 1977.

Bieri, Jurg & Schmitz, Andrew, Export Instability, Monopoly Power and Welfare. Journal of International Economics, No 9, 1976.

Bjork, Olle, Utvecklingen pa den internationella oljemarknaden. Skrift Nr 1978: 5 Forskningsgruppen for energisystemstudier, Nationalekonomiska Institutionen, Stockholms Universitet. (Development of the International Aid Market. Doc. 1978: 5, The Research Group on Energy Studies. The Institution of Economics, University of Stockholm.)

Black, Jan Knippers, United States' Penetration of Brazil. Manchester University Press 1977.

Blair, John M., The Control of Oil, Pantheon 1976.

Blum, J. M., V was for Victory. Politics and American Culture During World War II. Harcourt Brace Jovanovich. New York and London.

Bosson, Rex & Varon, Benison, The Mining Industry and the Developing Countries. Oxford University Press 1977.

Brecher, Irving & Abbas, S. A., Foreign Aid and Industrial Development in Pakistan.

Brook, Ezriel & Grilli, Enzo R., Commodity Price Stabilization and the Developing World. Finance and Development, No 1, March 1977. (This article is a summary of a comprehensive study made by the World Bank.)

Bunche, Ralph J., Trusteeship and Non-Self-Governing Territories in the Charter of the United Nations. Department of State, Bulletin Vol XIII, No 340, December 1945.

Bunte, Rune & Jorberg, Lennart, Historia i siffror. CWK Gleerup Bokfrlag. Lund. (History in figures.)

Byres, T. J. (ed), Foreign Resources and Economic Development. A Symposium on the report of the Pearson Commission. Frank Cass, London 1972.

Campbell, Bruce & Mytelka, Lynn K., Petrodollar Flows, Foreign Aid and International Stratification. Journal of World Trade Law, Vol 9, No 6, 1975.

Chydenius, Anders, Den nationale Winsten, wordsamt ofwerlamnad Til Riksens Hoflofliga Stander Af en Deras Ledamot. Tryckt hos Directeuren Lars Salvius 1765. Nytryck 1929 pa Kooperativa Forbundets Bokflorlag, Stockholm. (The National Profit, faithfully submitted to the Honorable Four Estates of the Realm by one of their Members.)

van Cleveland, Harold B. & Brittain, W. H. Bruce, Are the LDCs in over their heads? Foreign Affairs, Vol 55, No 4, July 1977.

Condliffe, J. B., The Commerce of Nations. George Allen and Unwin Ltd. London 1951.

Cooper, Richard, An Economic Order for Mutual Gain from Foreign Policy, No 26 1977.

Coppock, Joseph D., International Economic Instability. McGraw Hill, New York 1962.

Deakin, B. M., Shipping Conferences. A Study of their Origins, Development and Economic Practices. University of Cambridge. Department of Applied Economics. Occasional Paper No 37. Cambridge University Press 1973.

Dell, Sidney, Handelsblock och marknader. Raben & Sjogren. Stockholm 1965. (Trade blocs and Common Markets. Alfred A. Knopf, New York 1963.)

Dillard, Dudley, Vasteuropas och Forenta Staternas ekonomiska historia. Gleerups. Lund 1970. (Economic Development of the North Atlantic Community. A Historical Introduction to Modern Economics. Prentice Hall Englewood Cliffs 1967.)

Development Forum, March 1978. UN Centre for Economic and Social

Information.

Ekundare, R. Olufemi, An Economic History of Nigeria 1860-1960. Methuen & Co. London 1973.

Elliot, William Y., Freedom and Responsibility in Strausz-Hupe (1958).

Ellsworth, P. T., The International Economy. Third Edition. Macmillan Company. New York 1965.

Ensor, Richard, The American Economy: A Reappraisal. The Hudson Letter: A Special Report. Hudson Research Europe Ltd. Paris 1978.

Erb, G. F. & Schiavo-Campo, Salvatore, Export Instability, Level of Development and Economic Size of Less Developed Countries. Bulletin of the Oxford University, November 1969.

Ewing, A. F., UNCTAD and the Transfer of Technology. Journal of World Trade Law, Vol 10, No 3 1976.

Farer, Tom J., The United States and the Third World: A Basis for Acommodation. Foreign Affairs 54, October 1975.

Fasbender, Karl & Wagner, Wolfgang, Shipping Conferences, Rate Policy and Developing Countries. Verlag Weltarkiv, Hamburg 1973.

Ferry, Jules, Tonkin et la Mere Patrie in Fieldhouse (1967).

Fieldhouse, D. K., The Theory of Capitalist Imperialism. Longman. London 1967.

———— The Colonial Empires. A Comparative Survey from the Eighteenth Century. Weidenfeld and Nicolson. London 1971.

———— Economics and Empire 1830-1914. Weidenfeld and Nicolson. London 1973.

Fong, Pan Eng & Lim, Linda, The Electronics Industry in Singapore: Structure Technology and Linkages. Economic Research Centre. University of Singapore. ERC Monograph Series No 7. Chopmen Enterprises.

Furtado, Celso, Economic Development of Latin America. A survey from colonial times to the Cuban revolution. Cambridge University Press 1970.

Galtung, Johan, Poor Countries vs Rich; Poor People vs Rich. Whom Will NIEO Benefit? University of Oslo and Institut Universitaire d'Etudes de Developpement, Geneva. Stencil.

Gardner, Richard N., In Pursuit of World Order. Frederick A. Praeger, New York 1964.

GATT: International Trade 1973/74. Geneva 1974.

———— 1977/78. Geneva 1978.

Gordon, Wendell C., The Political Economy of Latin America. Columbia University Press. New York and London 1965.

Gould, J. D., Economic Growth in History. Methuen & Co Ltd. London 1972.

Griffin, Keith, Reform and Diversification in a Coffee Economy: The Case of Guatemala in Paul Streeten, ed. Unfashionable Economics. Weidenfeld and Nicolson, London 1970.

—— The Political Economy of Agrarian Change. An Essay on the Green Revolution. Harvard University Press. Cambridge, Massachusetts 1974.

Grjebine, Andre, Du desendettement du tiers monde a la regulation de la conjuncture mondiale . . . Quelques propositions. Problems Internationaux. No 362. Mai 1977.

Grubel, Harry, The Case Against an International Commodity Reserve Currency, Oxford Economic Papers. N.S. 17, No 1, March 1965.

Grubel, H. G., The Case against the New International Economic Order. Weltwirtschaftliches Archiv. Review of World Economics. Band 113, Heft 2, 1977.

Haellkvist, Karl Reinhold & Sanden-Haellkvist, Inger, Indiens, Pakistans och Bangladesh' historia. Studentlitteratur. Malmo 1973. (The History of India, Pakistan and Bangladesh.)

Halperin, Maurice, Growth and Crisis in the Latin American Economy in Petras & Zeitlin (1968).

Haq, Mahbub ul, The Poverty Curtain. Choices of the Third World. Columbia University Press, New York 1976.

Harris, Seymour m fl, Appraisals of Russian Economic Statistics, Review of Economic Statistics. XXIX, No 4, November 1947.

Hart, Albert G., Kaldor, Nicholas & Tinbergen, Jan, The Case for an International Commodity Reserve Currency. UNCTAD E/Conf 46/P/7, February 17, 1964.

Heaver, Trevor D., A Theory of Shipping Conference Pricing and Policies. Maritime Studies and Management. Vol 1, July 1973.

Heppling, Sixten, FN och de fattiga landerna. Prisma, Stockholm 1970. (The United Nations and the Poor Countries.)

Hermele, Kenneth & Larsson, Karl Anders, Solidaritet eller imperialism. Om Sverige, varldsordningen och Tredje varlden. Liber Forlag, Stockholm 1977. (Solidarity or Imperialism. On Sweden, the World Order and the Third World.)

Hilgerdt, Folke, Industrialization and Foreign Trade. League of Nations, Geneva 1945.

Hobsbawm, E. J., Industry and Empire. Penguin Books 1969.

—— The Age of Capital 1848–1875. Charles Scribner's Sons. New York 1975.

Hopkins, A. G., An Economic History of West Africa. Columbia University Press. New York 1973.

Hudson, Michael, Superimperialism — the Economic Strategy of American Empire. Holt, Rinehart and Winston. New York 1972.

——— Global Fracture, The New International Economic Order. Harper & Row Publishers. New York 1977.

Hughes, Jonathan, Industrialization and Economic History: Thesis and Conjectures. McGraw Hill Book Company. New York 1970.

Hunter, Guy, The Best of Both Worlds? Oxford University Press. London 1967 quoted in Rothstein (1977).

IBRD, The Problem of Stabilization of Prices of Primary Products, 1968.

——— Trends in Developing Countries, 1973.

——— World Development Report, 1978.

ILO: Employment, Growth and Basic Needs. A One-World Problem. Geneva 1976.

Internationella koncerner i industrilander. Betankande av koncentrations-utredningen. SOU 1975: 50. (Transnational Corporations in Industrialised Countries.)

James, Robert Rhodes, The British Revolution 1880-1939. Alfred A. Knopf, New York 1977.

Jankiwitsch, O. & Sauvant, K., The Evolution of the Non-Aligned Movement into a Pressure Group for the Establishment of a New International Economic Order. Prepared for delivery at the XVII Annual Convention of the International Studies Association, Toronto 25–29 February 1976.

Johnson, Harry G., Economic Policies Toward Less Developed Countries. Frederick A. Praeger. New York 1967.

Karunatilake, H. N. S., Economic Development in Ceylon. Praeger Publishers. New York 1971.

Kenwood, A. G. & Lougheed, A. L., The Growth of the International Economy 1820-1960. George Allen & Unwin Ltd. London 1971.

Kindleberger, Charles, Power and Money — the Economics of International Politics and the Politics of International Economics. Macmillan. London 1970.

King, G. J., The New International Economic Order. Behind the Headlines, Vol XXXIV, No 5, 1976. The Canadian Institute of International Affairs.

Knudsen, Odin & Parnes, Andrew, Trade Instability and Economic Development: An Empirical Study. Lexington Books. Lexington 1975.

Kofi, Tetteh A., The International Cocoa Agreements, Journal of World Trade Law, Vol 11, No 1, Jan–Feb 1977.

Kolko, Gabriel, The Politics of War. The World and United States Foreign Policy 1943–45. Vintage Books. New York 1970.

——— Amerikansk utrikespolitik. Raben & Sjogren. Stockholm 1970. (The Roots of American Foreign Policy. An Analysis of Power and Purpose. Beacon Press. Boston.)

Krenin, Mordechai & Finger, J. M., A Critical Survey of the New International Economic Order. Journal of World Trade Law, Vol 10, No 6, 1976.

Kuznets, Simon, Economic Growth and Structure. Heinemann. London 1965.

—— Modern Economic Growth. Rate Structure and Spread. Yale University Press. New Haven and London 1966.

—— Economic Growth of Nations. Harvard University Press. Cambridge, Massachusetts 1971.

—— Problems in comparing recent growth rates for developed and less developed countries. Economic Development and Cultural Change, 20, No 2, January 1972.

Lall, Sanjaya, The Patent System and the Transfer of Technology to Less-Developed Countries. Journal of World Trade Law, Vol 10, No 1, 1976.

Lall, Sanjaya & Streeten, Paul, Foreign Investments, Transnationals and Developing Countries. Macmillan Press Ltd. London 1977.

Lary, Hal and Associates, The United States in the World Economy. U.S. Department of Commerce. Series No 23. Washington 1943.

Ledogar, Robert J., Hungry for Profits: US Food & Drug Multinationals in Latin America. IDOC/North America. New York 1975.

Letelier, O. & Moffitt, M., The International Economic Order, Part 1. Transnational Institute, Pamphlet no 2. Washington 1977.

Lundahl, Mats, En utopisk varldsordning and andra essaer om ekonomisk utveckling och underutveckling. Raben & Sjogren. Stockholm 1978. (A Utopian World Order and Other Essays about Economic Development and Underdevelopment.)

MacBean, Alasdair I., Export Instability and Economic Development. Georg Allen & Unwin. London 1966.

Machlup, Fritz, International Monetary Economics. George Allen & Unwin. London 1966.

Maddison, Angus, Economic Growth in the West. New York 1964.

—— Economic Progress and Policy in Developing Countries. George Allen & Unwin Ltd. London 1970.

—— Class Structure and Economic Growth. India & Pakistan since the Maghuls. George Allen & Unwin. London 1971.

Mason, Edward S. & Asher, Robert E., The World Bank Since Bretton Woods. The Brookings Institution. Washington, D.C. 1973.

Massell, Benton F., Price Stabilization and Welfare. Quarterly Journal of Economics, No 83, May 1969.

—— Export Instability and Economic Structure. American Economic Revuew, Vol 60, September 1970.

Mauro, Frederic: Historie de l'economie mondiale. Editions Sirey. Paris

1971.

Mates, Leo, The Nonaligned Countries between Colombo and Havanna. Pacific Community–Asian Quarterly Review, April 1978, pp. 291–301.

McNeill, William H., Plagues and People, Anchor Press/Doubleday, New York 1976.

Mende, Tibor, De L'aide a la recolonisation. Les lecons d'un echec. Editions du Seuil. Paris 1972.

Mendis, Vernon, The Policy of Non-Alignment. Marga Quarterly Journal, Vol 3, No 3, 1976, pp. 31–45.

Menon, Bhaskar, Global Dialogue – The New International Economic Order. Pergamon Press 1977.

Mill, John Stuart, Principles of Political Economy (1848, 7th Edition 1871) in Fieldhouse (1976).

Morton, Kathryn & Tulloch, Peter, Trade and Developing Countries. Croom Helm. London 1977.

Moller, Birger, Ny ekonomisk varldsordnung? Varldspolitikens dagsfragor, Nr 7, 1976. Utrikespolitiska Institutet. (A New International Economic Order?)

Nayyar, Deepak, Transnational Corporations and Manufactured Exports from Poor Countries. Economic Journal, 88, March 1978.

Nirumand, Bahman, Shahens Persien. Raben & Sjogren. Stockholm 1968. (The Persia of the Shah.)

Non-Alignment & Third World Solidarity, Marga Quarterly Journal, Special Issue Vol 3, No 3, 1976.

Odell, Peter R., Oil and World Power – Background to the Oil Crises. Penguin, Fourth edition 1975.

OECD, DAC Chairman Report 1977. Paris 1977.

Panikkar, K. M., Asia and Western Dominance. George Allen & Unwin. London 1953.

Perez-Guerrero, Manuel, The New International Economic Order and the International Law. Speech at the 20th Seminar for Diplomats in Salzburg 1 August 1977. Stencil.

Perham, Margery, The British Problem in Africa. Foreign Affairs, Vol XXIX 1951.

Pincus, John A., The Cost of Foreign Aid. Review of Economics and Statistics. Vol 45, November 1963.

Prebisch, Raul, Towards a New Strategy for Development. UNCTAD. Geneva 1964.

——— Development Problems in Latin America. University of Texas, Austin 1970.

Radetzki, Marian, En ny ekonomisk varldsordnung. Esselte Studium. Lund 1976. (A New International Economic World Order.)

Radice, Hugo, International Firms and Modern Imperialism. Penguin Books 1975.

Raghavan, Chaleravathi, The Promises of Havana. IFDA Dossier 13 November 1979.

Resources and Man — A Study and Recommendations Committee on Resources and Man. National Academy of Sciences — National Research Council. W.H. Freeman and Company. San Francisco 1969.

Resurserna, Samhallet och framtiden. Slutrapport fran projektet Resurser och ravaror. Sekretariatet for framtidsstudier. Liber Forlag. Stockholm 1977. (Resources, Society and the Future.)

Robinson, Austin, Fifty Years of Commonwealth Economic Development. Smuts Memorial Lecture. Cambridge University Press 1972.

Rothstein, Robert L., Foreign Policy and Development Policy: From Non-alignment to International Class War. International Affairs, October 1976, pp. 598–616.

—— The Weak in the World of the Strong. The Developing Countries in the International System. Columbia University Press. New York 1977.

Routh, Guy, The Origin of economic Ideas. Vintage Books. New York 1977.

Saul, S. B., Studies in British Overseas Trade 1870-1914. London 1960.

Sauvant, K. & Hassenflug, H. (eds), The New International Economic Order. Wilton House Publications. London Westview Press 1977.

Schiavo-Campo, Salvatore & Singer, Hans, Perspectives of Economic Development. Houghton Mifflin Company. New York 1970.

Schultz, T. W., Value of U.S. Farm Surpluses to Underdeveloped Countries. Journal of Farm Economics. Vol 62, December 1962.

Servoise, René, New Third World Strategy: Solidarity, not Charity. Manchester Guardian and Le Monde, May 23, 1976. Quoted in Hudson (1977).

Silk, Leonard, Capitalism: the moving target. Quadrangle. The New York International Times Book Co. New York 1974.

Singer, H. H., International Development: Growth and Change. McGraw Hill, New York 1964.

Solomon, Robert, The International Monetary System 1945-76. An Insider's View. Harper & Row Publishers. New York 1977.

Spector, I., The First Russian Revolution. Its Impact on Asia. Englewood Cliffs 1962.

Stern, Fritz, Gold and Iron. Bismarch, Bleichroder and the Building of the German Empire. Alfred A. Knopf. New York 1977.

Strausz-Hupe, Robert & Hazard, Harry W., The Idea of Colonialism. Frederick A. Praeger. New York 1958.

Survey of International Development, March/April 1975. Society for International Development.

Svedberg, Peter, Den gamla varldsordningen. (Stencil) 1977. (The Old World Order.)

——— Svensk u-landspolitik under omprovning. Ekonomisk Debatt, Nr 6, 1978. (Swedish Aid Policy under Reconsideration.)

Sveriges samarbete med u-landerna. Betankande av bistandspolitiska utredningen. SOU 1977: 13. Bilagor i SOU 1977: 14. (Sweden's Cooperation with Developing Countries.)

Szentes, Tamás, The Political Economy of Underdevelopment. Akadémiai Kiadó. Budapest 1973.

Sodersten, Bo, Internationell ekonomi. Raben & Sjogren. Stockholm 1969. (International Economy.)

Teece, D.J., The Multinational Corporation and the Resource Cost of International Technology Transfer. Ballinger Publishing Company. Cambridge, Massachusetts 1976.

——— Technology Transfer by Multinational Firms: The Resource Cost of Transferring Know How. Economic Journal 87, June 1977.

Tew, Brian, The Evolution of the International Monetary System 1945–77. Hutchinson of London 1977.

The Times History of Our Times, Editor Marcus Cunliffe. Weidenfeld and Nicolson. London 1971.

Trilateral Commission. Task Force Reports: 9–14. The Triangle Papers. New York University Press. New York 1978.

Tucker, Robert W., The Inequality of Nations. Basic Books. New York 1977.

UNCTAD, Import Cooperation among Developing Countries. TD/8/AC. 19/R.4. Geneva 1975.

——— The International Patent System as an Instrument of Policy for National Development. TD/B/C.6/AC.2/3. July 1975.

——— Handbook of International Trade and Development Statistics 1976. United Nations TD/Stat 6. New York 1976.

——— Handbook of International Trade and Development Statistics 1979. TD/Stat 8. New York 1979.

UNIDO, Industrial Development Survey. Special issue for the Second General Conference of UNIDO. ID/CONF. 3/2. New York 1974.

UNITAR, A New International Economic Order. Selected Documents 1945–75. Vol I & II. Compiled by Moss, A. G., & Winton, H. N. M. Document Service No 1.

United Nations, Relative Prices of Exports and Imports of Under-developed Countries. New York 1949.

——— Post-War Price Relations between Underdeveloped and Industrialized Countries. February 1949.

——— Instability in Export Markets of Underdeveloped Countries. New York 1962.

——— Multinational Corporations in World Development 1973.

——— Transnational Corporations in World Development: A Re-Examination. E/C.10/38. 20 March 1978.

Vaitsos, Constantine V., Intercountry Income Distribution and Transnational Enterprises. Clarendon Press, Oxford 1974.

Weber, Max, General Economic History. Collier–Macmillan. New York 1966.

Weissman, Steve, The Trojan Horse. A Radical Look at Foreign Aid. Ramparts Press. San Francisco 1974.

White, John, The Politics of Foreign Aid. The Bodley Head. London 1974.

Whitman, Marina V. N., The Payments Adjustment Process and the Exchange Rate Regime: What Have We Learned. American Economic Review. Vol LXV, May 1975, No 2.

Wijkman, Per Magnus, Svensk flagg i motvind. Ekonomisk Debatt 1977: 3. (Swedish Flag against the Wind.)

Willrich, Mason, Energy and World Politics. Published under the auspices of the American Society of International Law. The Free Press 1975.

Wilkins, Myra, The Emergence of Multinational Enterprise. American Business Abroad from the Colonial Era to 1914. Harvard University Press. Cambridge, Massachusetts 1970.

——— The Maturing of Multinational Enterprises: American Business from 1914 to 1970. Harvard University Press. Cambridge, Massachusetts 1975.

Wilkinson, Richard G., Poverty and Progress. An Ecological Perspective on Economic Development. Praeger Publishers. New York, Washington 1973.

Winch, Donald, Classical Political Economy and Colonies. G. Bell and Sons Ltd. London 1965.

Wolff, Richard D., The Economics of Colonialism. Britain and Kenya 1870–1930. Yale University Press. New Haven and London 1974.

Worland, Stephen T., Justum pretium: one more round in an 'endless series'. History of Political Economy, Vol 9, No 4, Winter 1977.

Yates, Lamartine, Forty Years of Foreign Trade. London 1959.

Yeats, Alexander J., Monopoly Power, Barriers to competition and the Pattern of Price Differentials in International Trade. Institute for International Studies. University of Stockholm. Reprint Series No 94.

——— Do International Costs Increase with Fabrication? Some Empirical Evidence. Institute for International Studies. University of Stockholm. Reprint Series No 87.

Yotopoulos, Pan A. & Nugent, Jeffry, Economics of Development. Harper & Row. New York 1976.

APPENDIX 1

3201 (S-V1). Declaration on the Establishment of a New International Economic Order

The General Assembly
Adopts the following Declaration:

DECLARATION ON THE ESTABLISHMENT OF A NEW INTERNATIONAL ECONOMIC ORDER

We, the Members of the United Nations,

Having convened a special session of the General Assembly to study for the first time the problems of raw materials and development, devoted to the consideration of the most important economic problems facing the world ecommunity,

Bearing in mind the spirit, purposes and principles of the Charter of the United Nations to promote the economic advancement and social progress of all peoples,

Solemnly proclaim our united determination to work urgently for THE ESTABLISHMENT OF A NEW INTERNATIONAL ECONOMIC ORDER based on equity, sovereign equality, interdependence, common interest and cooperation among all States, irrespective of their economic and social systems which shall correct inequalities and redress existing injustices, make is possible to eliminate the widening gap between the developed and the developing countries and ensure steadily accelerating economic and social development and peace and justice for present and future generations, and, to that end, declare:

1. The greatest and most significant achievement during the last decades has been the independence from colonial and alien domination of a large

number of peoples and nations which has enabled them to become members of the community of free peoples. Technological progress has also been made in all speheres of economic activities in the last three decades, thus providing a solid potential for improving the well-being of all peoples. However, the remaining vestiges of alien and colonial domination, foreign occupation, racial discrimination, *apartheid* and neo-colonialism in all its forms to be among the greatest obstacles to the full emancipation and progress of the developing countries and all the peoples involved. The benefits of technological progress are not shared equitable by all members of the international community. The developing countries, which constitute 70 per cent of the world's population, account for only 30 per cent of the world's income. It has proved impossible to achieve an even and balanced development of the international community under the existing international economic order. The gap between the developed and the developing countries continues to widen in a system which was established at a time when most of the developing countries did not even exist as independent States and which perpetuates inequality.

2. The present international economic order is in direct conflict with current developments in international political and economic relations. Since 1970, the world economy has experienced a series of grave crises which have had severe repercussions, especially on the developing countries because of their generally greater vulnerability to external economic impulses. The developing world has become a powerful factor that makes its influence felt in all fields of international activity. These irreversible changes in the relationship of forces in the world necessitate the active, full and equal participation of the developing countries in the formulation and application of all decisions that concern the international community.

3. All these changes have thrust into prominence the reality of interdependence of all the members of the world community. Current events have brought into sharp focus the realization that the interests of the developed countries and those of the developing countries can no longer be isolated from each other, that there is a close interrelationship between the prosperity of the developed countries and the growth and development of the developing countries, and that the prosperity of the international community as a whole depends upon the prosperity of its constituent parts. International co-operation for development is the shared goal and common duty of all countries. Thus the political, economic and social well-being of present and future generations depends more than ever on co-operation between all the members of the international community on the basis of sovereign equality and the removal of the disequilibrium that exists between them.

4. The new international economic order should be founded on full

respect for the following principles:

(*a*)   Sovereign equality of States, self-determination of all peoples, inadmissibility of the acquisition of territories by force, territorial integrity and non-interference in the internal affairs of other States;

(*b*)   The broadest co-operation of all the States members of the international community, based on equity, whereby the prevailing disparities in the world may be banished and prosperity secured for all;

(*c*)   Full and effective participation on the basis of equality of all countries in the solving of world economic problems in the common interest of all countries, bearing in mind the necessity to ensure the accelerated development of all the developing countries, while devoting particular attention to the adoption of special measures in favour of the least developed, land-locked and island developing countries as well as those developing countries most seriously affected by economic crises and natural calamities, without losing sight of the interests of other developing countries;

(*d*)   The right of every country to adopt the economic and social system that it deems the most appropriate for its own development and not to be subject to discrimination of any kind as a result;

(*e*)   Full permanent sovereignty of every State over its natural resources and all economic activities. In order to safeguard these resources, each State is entitled to exercise effective control over them and their exploitation with means suitable to its own situation, including the right to nationalization or transfer of ownership to its nationals, this right being an expression of the full permanent sovereignty of the State. No State may be subjected to economic, political or any other type of coercion to prevent the free and full exercise of this inalienable right;

(*f*)   The right of all States, territories and peoples under foreign occupation, alien and colonial domination or *apartheid* to restitution and full compensation for the exploitation and depletion of, and damages to, the natural resources and all other resources of those States, territories and peoples;

(*g*)   Regulation and supervision of the activities of transnational corporations by taking measures in the interest of the national economies of the countries where such transnational corporations operate on the basis of the full sovereignty of those countries;

(*h*)   The right of the developing countries and the peoples of territories under colonial and racial domination and foreign occupation to achieve their liberation and to regain effective control over their natural resources and economic activities;

(*i*)   The extending of assistance to developing countries, peoples and territories which are under colonial and alien domination, foreign occupation, racial discrimination or *apartheid* or are subjected to economic, political or any other type of coercive measures to obtain from them the subordination of the exercise of their sovereign rights and to secure from them advantages of any kind, and to neo-colonialism in all its forms, and which have established or are endeavouring to establish effective control over their natural resources and economic activities that have been or are still under foreign control;

(*j*) Just and equitable relationship between the prices of raw materials, primary commodities, manufactured and semi-manufactured goods exported by developing countries and the prices of raw materials, primary commodities, manufactures, capital goods and equipment imported by them with the aim of bringing about sustained improvement in their unsatisfactory terms of trade and the expansion of the world economy;

(*k*) Extension of active assistance to developing countries by the whole international community, free of any political or military conditions;

(*l*) Ensuring that one of the main aims of the reformed international monetary system shall be the promotion of the development of the developing countries and the adequate flow of real resources to them;

(*m*) Improving the competitiveness of natural materials facing competition from synthetic substitutes;

(*n*) Preferential and non-reciprocal treatment for developing countries, wherever feasible, in all fields of international economic co-operation whenever possible;

(*o*) Securing favourable conditions for the transfer of financial resources to developing countries;

(*p*) Giving to the developing countries access to the achievements of modern science and technology, and promoting the transfer of technology and the creation of indigenous technology for the benefit of the developing countries in forms and in accordance with procedures which are suited to their economies;

(*q*) The need for all States to put an end to the waste of natural resources, including food products;

(*r*) The need for developing countries to concentrate all their resources for the cause of development;

(*s*) The strengthening, though individual and collective actions, of mutual economic, trade, financial and technical co-operation among the developing countries, mainly on a preferential basis;

(*t*) Facilitating the role which producers' associations may play within the framework of international co-operation and, in pursuance of their aims, *inter alia* assisting in the promotion of sustained growth of the world economy and accelerating the development of developing countries.

5. The unanimous adoption of the International Development Strategy for the Second United Nations Development Decade[5] was an important step in the promotion of international economic co-operation on a just and equitable basis. The accelerated implementation of obligations and commitments assumed by the international community within the framework of the Strategy, particularly those concerning imperative development needs of developing countries, would contribute significantly to the fulfilment of the aims and objectives of the present Declaration.

6. The United Nations as a universal organization should be capable of dealing with problems of international economic co-operation in a comprehensive manner and ensuring equally the interests of all countries. It must have an even greater role in the establishment of a new international economic order. The Charter of Economic Rights and Duties of States, for the preparation of which the present Declaration will provide an additional source of inspiration, will constitute a significant contribution in this respect. All the States Members of the United Nations are therefore called upon to exert maximum efforts with a view to securing the implementation of the present Declaration, which is one of the principal guarantees for the creation of better conditions for all peoples to reach a life worthy of human dignity.

7. The present Declaration on the Establishment of a new International Economic Order shall be one of the most important bases of economic relations between all peoples and all nations.

2229th plenary meeting
1 May 1974

3202 (S–VI). Programme of Action on the Establishment of a New International Economic Order

The General Assembly
Adopts the following Programme of Action:

PROGRAMME OF ACTION ON THE ESTABLISHMENT OF A NEW INTERNATIONAL ECONOMIC ORDER

CONTENTS

5. Resolution 2626 (XXV).

. INTRODUCTION

1. In view of the continuing severe economic imbalance in the relations between developed and developing countries, and in the context of the constant and continuing aggravation of the imbalance of the economies of the developing countries and the consequent need for the mitigation of their current economic difficulties, urgent and effective measures need to be taken by the international community to assist the developing countries, while devoting particular attention to the least developed, land-locked and island developing countries and those developing countries most seriously affected by economic crises and natural calamities leading to serious retardation of development processes.

2. With a view to ensuring the application of the Declaration on the Establishment of a New International Economic Order,[6] it will be necessary to adopt and implement within a specified period a programme of action of unprecedented scope and to bring about maximum economic co-operation and understanding among all States, particularly between developed and developing countries, based on the principles of dignity and sovereign equality.

I.   FUNDAMENTAL PROBLEMS OF RAW MATERIALS AND PRIMARY
      COMMODITIES AS RELATED TO TRADE AND DEVELOPMENT

1. *Raw materials*

All efforts should be made:

(*a*)   To put an end to all forms of foreign occupation, racial discrimination, *apartheid*, colonial, neo-colonial and alien domination and exploitation through the exercise of permanent sovereignty over natural resources;

6. Resolution 3201 (S–VI).

(*b*)   To take measures for the recovery, exploitation, ddevelopment, marketing and distribution of natural resources, particularly of developing countries, to serve their national interests, to promote collective self-reliance among them and to strengthen mutually beneficial international economic co-operation with a view to bringing about the accelerated development of developing countries;

(*c*)   To facilitate the functioning and to further the aims of producers' associations, including their joint marketing arrangements, orderly commodity trading, improvement in the export income of producing developing countries and in their terms of trade, and sustained growth of the world economy for the benefit of all;

(*d*)   To evolve a just and equitable relationship between the price of raw materials, primary commodities, manufactured and semi-manufactured goods exported by developing countries and the prices of raw materials, primary commodities, food, manufactured and semi-manufactured goods and capital equipment imported by them, and to work for a link between the prices of exports of developing countries and the prices of their imports from developed countries;

(*e*)   To take measures to reverse the continued trend of stagnation or decline in the real price of several commodities exported by developing countries, despite a general rise in commodity prices, resulting in a decline in the export earnings of these developing countries;

(*f*)   To take measures to expand the markets for natural products in relation to synthetics, taking into account the interests of the developing countries, and to utilize fully the ecological advantages of these products;

(*g*)   To take measures to promote the processing of raw materials in the producer developing countries.

2.   *Food*

All efforts should be made:

(*a*)   To take full account of specific problems of developing countries, particularly in times of food shortages, in the international efforts connected with the food problem;

(*b*)   To take into account that, owing to lack of means, some developing countries have vast potentialities of unexploited or underexploited land which, if reclaimed and put into practical use, would contribute considerably to the solution of the food crisis;

(*c*)   By the international community to undertake concrete and speedy measures with a view to arresting desertification, salination and damage by locusts or any other similar phenomenon involving several developing countries, particularly in Africa, and gravely affecting the agricultural production capacity of these countries, and also to assist the developing countries affected by any such phenomenon to develop the affected zones with a view to contributing to the solution of their food problems;

(*d*) To refrain from damaging or deteriorating natural resources and food resources, especially those derived from the sea, by preventing pollution and taking appropriate steps to protect and reconstitute those resources;

(*e*) By developed countries, in evolving their policies relating to production, stocks, imports and exports of food, to take full account of the interests of:

(i) Developing importing countries which cannot afford high prices for their imports;

(ii) Developing exporting countries which need increased market opportunities for their exports;

(*f*) To ensure that developing countries can import the necessary quantity of food without undue strain on their foreign exchange resources and without unpredictable deterioration in their balance of payments, and, in this context, that special measures are taken in respect of the least developed, land-locked and island developing countries as well as those developing countries most seriously affected by economic crises and natural calamities;

(*g*) To ensure that concrete measures to increase food production and storage facilities in developing countries are introduced, *inter alia*, by ensuring an increase in all available essential inputs, including fertilizers, from developed countries on favourable terms;

(*h*) To promote exports of food products of developing countries through just and equitable arrangements, *inter alia*, by the progressive elimination of such protective and other measures as constitute unfair competition.

3. *General trade*

All efforts should be made:

(*a*) To take the following measures for the amelioration of terms of trade of developing countries and concrete steps to eliminate chronic trade deficits of developing countries;

(i) Fulfilment of relevant commitments already undertaken in the United Nations Conference on Trade and Development and in the International Development Strategy for the Second United Nations Development Decade;[7]

(ii) Improved access to markets in developed countries through the progressive removal of tariff and non-tariff barriers and of

7. Resolution 2626 (XXV).

restrictive business practices;

(iii) Expeditious formulation of commodity agreements where appropriate, in order to regulate as necessary and to stabilize the world markets for raw materials and primary commodities;

(iv) Preparation of an over-all integrated programme, setting out guidelines and taking into account the current work in this field, for a comprehensive range of commodities of export interest to developing countries;

(v) Where products of developing countries compete with the domestic production in developed countries, each developed country should facilitate the expansion of imports from developing countries and provide a fair and reasonable opportunity to the developing countries to share in the growth of the market;

(vi) When the importing developed countries derive receipts from customs duties, taxes and other protective measures applied to imports of these products, consideration should be given to the claim of the developing countries that these receipts should be reimbursed in full to the exporting developing countries or devoted to providing additional resources to meet their development needs;

(vii) Developed countries should make appropriate adjustments in their economies so as to facilitate the expansion and diversification of imports from developing countries and thereby permit a rational, just and equitable international division of labour;

(viii) Setting up general principles for pricing policy for exports of commodities of developing countries, with a view to rectifying and achieving satisfactory terms of trade for them;

(ix) Until satisfactory terms of trade are achieved for all developing countries, consideration should be given to alternative means, including improved compensatory financing schemes for meeting the development needs of the developing countries concerned;

(x) Implementation, improvement and enlargement of the generalized system of preferences for exports of agricultural primary commodities, manufactures and semi-manufactures from developing to developed countries and consideration of its extension to commodities, including those which are processed; developing countries which are or will be sharing their existing tariff advantages in some developed countries as the result of the introduction and eventual enlargement of the generalized system of preferences should, as a matter of urgency, be granted new openings in the markets of other developed countries which should offer them export opportunities that at least compensate for the sharing of those advantages;

(xi) The setting up of buffer stocks within the framework of commodity arrangements and their financing by international financial institutions, wherever necessary, by the developed countries and when they are able to do so, by the developing countries, with the aim of favouring the producer developing and consumer developing countries and of contributing to the expansion of world trade as a whole;

(xii) In cases where natural materials can satisfy the requirements of the market, new investment for the expansion of the capacity to produce synthetic materials and substitutes should not be made;

(b) To be guided by the principles of non-reciprocity and preferential treatment of developing countries in multilateral trade negotiations between developed and developing countries, and to seek sustained and additional benefits for the international trade of developing countries, so as to achieve a substantial increase in their foreign exchange earnings, diversification of their exports and acceleration of the rate of their economic growth.

4.   *Transportation and insurance*

All efforts should be made:

(a)   To promote an increasing and equitable participation of developing countries in the world shipping tonnage;

(b)   To arrest and reduce the ever-increasing freight rates in order to reduce the costs of imports to, and exports from, the developing countries;

(c)   To minimize the cost of insurance and reinsurance for developing countries and to assist the growth of domestic insurance and reinsurance markets in developing countries and the establishment to this end, where appropriate, of institutions in these countries or at the regional level;

(d)   To ensure the early implementation of the code of conduct for liner conferences;

(e)   To take urgent measures to increase the import and export capability of the least developed countries and to offset the disadvantages of the adverse geographic situation of land-locked countries, particularly with regard to their transportation and transit costs, as well as developing island countries in order to increase their trading ability;

(f)   By the developed countries to refrain from imposing measures or implementing policies designed to prevent the importation, at equitable prices, of commodities from the developing countries or from frustrating the implementation of legitimate measures and policies adopted by the developing countries in order to improve prices and encourage the export of such commodities.

II.   INTERNATIONAL MONETARY SYSTEM AND FINANCING OF THE
DEVELOPMENT OF DEVELOPING COUNTRIES

1. *Objectives*

All efforts should be made to reform the international monetary system
with, *inter alia*, the following objectives:

(*a*)   Measures to check the inflation already experienced by the developed countries, to prevent it from being transferred to developing countries and to study and devise possible arrangements within the International
Monetary Fund to mitigate the effects of inflation in developed countries
on the economies of developing countries;

(*b*)   Measures to eliminate the instability of the international monetary system, in particular the uncertainty of the exchange rates, especially
as it affects adversely the trade in commodities;

(*c*)   Maintenance of the real value of the currency reserves of the
developing countries by preventing their erosion from inflation and
exchange rate depreciation of reserve currencies;

(*d*)   Full and effective participation of developing countries in all
phases of decision-making for the formulation of an equitable and durable
monetary system and adequate participation of developing countries in all
bodies entrusted with this reform and, particularly, in the proposed
Council of Governors of the International Monetary Fund;

(*e*)   Adequate and orderly creation of additional liquidity with particular regard to the needs of the developing countries through the additional allocation of special drawing rights based on the concept of world
liquidity needs to be appropriately revised in the light of the new international environment; any creation of international liquidity should be
made through international multilateral mechanisms;

(*f*)   Early establishment of a link between special drawing rights and
additional developing financing in the interest of developing countries,
consistent with the monetary characteristics of special drawing rights;

(*g*)   Review by the International Monetary Fund of the relevant provi-
sions in order to ensure effective participation by developing countries in
the decision-making process;

(*h*)   Arrangements to promote an increasing net transfer of real resources from the developed to the developing countries;

(*i*)   Review of the methods of operation of the International Monetary Fund, in particular the terms for both credit repayments and
'standby' arrangements, the system of compensatory financing, and the
terms of the financing of commodity buffer stocks, so as to enable the

developing countries to make more effective use of them.

2. *Measures*

All efforts should be made to take the following urgent measures to finance the development of developing countries and to meet the balance-of-payment crises in the developing world;

(a) Implementation at an accelerated pace by the developed countries of the time-bound programme, as already laid down in the International Development Strategy for the Second United Nations Development Decade, for the net amount of financial resource transfers to developing countries so as to meet and even to exceed the target of the Strategy;

(b) International financing institutions should effectively play their role as development financing banks without discrimination on account of the political or economic system of any member country, assistance being untied;

(c) More effective participation by developing countries, whether recipients or contributors, in the decision-making process in the competent organs of the International Bank for Reconstruction and Development and the International Development Association, through the establishment of a more equitable pattern of voting rights;

(d) Exemption, wherever possible, of the developing countries from all import and capital outflow controls imposed by the developed countries;

(e) Promotion of foreign investment, both public and private, from developed to developing countries in accordance with the needs and requirements in sectors of their economies as determined by the recipient countries;

(f) Appropriate urgent measures, including international action, should be taken to mitigate adverse consequences for the current and future development of developing countries arising from the burden of external debt contracted on hard terms;

(g) Debt renegotiation on a case-by-case basis with a view to concluding agreements on debt cancellation, moratorium, rescheduling or interest subsidization;

(h) International financial institutions should take into account the special situation of each developing country in reorienting their lending policies to suit these urgent needs; there is also need for improvement in practices of international financial institutions in regard to, *inter alia*, development financing and international monetary problems;

(i) Appropriate steps should be taken to give priority to the least developed, land-locked and island developing countries and to the countries most seriously affected by economic crises and natural calamities, in the availability of loans for development purposes which should include more favourable terms and conditions.

III.   INDUSTRIALIZATION

All efforts should be made by the international community to take measures to encourage the industrialization of the developing countries, and to this end:

(*a*)   The developed countries should respond favourably, within the framework of their official aid as well as international financial institutions, to the requests of developing countries for the financing of industrial projects;

(*b*)   The developed countries should encourage investors to finance industrial production projects, particularly export-oriented production, in developing countries, in agreement with the latter and within the context of their laws and regulations;

(*c*)   With a view to bringing about a new international economic structure which should increase the share of the developing countries in world industrial production, the developed countries and the agencies of the United Nations system, in co-operation with the developing countries, should contribute to setting up new industrial capacities including raw materials and commodity-transforming facilities as a matter of priority in the developing countries that produce those raw materials and commodities;

(*d*)   The international community should continue and expand, with the aid of the developed countries and the international institutions, the operational and instruction-oriented technical assistance programmes, including vocational training and management development of national personnel of the developing countries, in the light of their special development requirements.

IV.   TRANSFER OF TECHNOLOGY

All efforts should be made:

(*a*)   To formulate an international code of conduct for the transfer of technology corresponding to needs and conditions prevalent in developing countries;

(*b*)   To give access on improved terms to modern technology and to adapt that technology, as appropriate, to specific economic, social and ecological conditions and varying stages of development in developing countries;

(*c*)   To expand significantly the assistance from developed to developing countries in research and development programmes and in the creation of suitable indigenous technology;

(*d*)   To adapt commercial practices governing transfer of technology to the requirements of the developing countries and to prevent abuse of the rights of sellers;

(*e*)   To promote international co-operation in research and development in exploration and exploitation, conservation and the legitimate utilization of natural resources and all sources of energy.

In taking the above measures, the special needs of the least developed and land-locked countries should be borne in mind.

V.   REGULATION AND CONTROL OVER THE ACTIVITIES OF TRANSNATIONAL CORPORATIONS

All efforts should be made to formulate, adopt and implement an international code of conduct for transnational corporations:

(*a*)   To prevent interference in the internal affairs of the countries where they operate and their collaboration with racist regimes and colonial administrations;

(*b*)   To regulate their activities in host countries, to eliminate restrictive business practices and to conform to the national development plans and objectives of developing countries, and in this context facilitate, as necessary, the review and revision of previously concluded arrangements;

(*c*)   To bring about assistance, transfer of technology and management skills to developing countries on equitable and favourable terms;

(*d*)   To regulate the repatriation of the profits accruing from their operations, taking into account the legitimate interests of all parties concerned;

(*e*)   To promote reinvestment of their profits in developing countries.

VI.   CHARTER OF ECONOMIC RIGHTS AND DUTIES OF STATES

The Charter of Economic Rights and Duties of States, the draft of which is being prepared by a working group of the United Nations and which the General Assembly has already expressed the intention of adopting at its twenty-ninth regular session, shall constitute an effective instrument towards the establishment of a new system of international economic relations based on equity, sovereign equality, and interdependence of the interests of developed and developing countries. It is therefore of vital importance that the aforementioned Charter be adopted by the General Assembly at its twenty-ninth session.

VII.   PROMOTION OF CO-OPERATION AMONG DEVELOPING COUNTRIES

1. Collective self-reliance and growing co-operation among developing

countries will further strengthen their role in the new international economic order. Developing countries, with a view to expanding co-operation at the regional, subregional and interregional levels, should take further steps, *inter alia*:

(*a*)   To support the establishment and/or improvement of an appropriate mechanism to defend the prices of their exportable commodities and to improve access to and stabilize markets for them. In this context the increasingly effective mobilization by the whole group of oil-exporting countries of their natural resources for the benefit of their economic development is to be welcomed. At the same time there is the paramount need for co-operation among the developing countries in evolving urgently and in a spirit of solidarity all possible means to assist developing countries to cope with the immediate problems resulting from this legitimate and perfectly justified action. The measures already taken in this regard are a positive indication of the evolving co-operation between developing countries;

(*b*)   To protect their inalienable right to permanent sovereignty over their natural resources;

(*c*)   To promote, establish or strengthen economic integration at the regional and subregional levels;

(*d*)   To increase considerably their imports from other developing countries;

(*e*)   To ensure that no developing country accords to imports from developed countries more favourable treatment than that accorded to imports from developing countries. Taking into account the existing international agreements, current limitations and possibilities and also their future evolution, preferential treatment should be given to the procurement of import requirements from other developing countries. Wherever possible, preferential treatment should be given to imports from developing countries and the exports of those countries;

(*f*)   To promote close co-operation in the fields of finance, credit relations and monetary issues, including the development of credit relations on a preferential basis and on favourable terms;

(*g*)   To strengthen efforts which are already being made by developing countries to utilize available financial resources for financing development in the developing countries through investment, financing of export-oriented and emergency projects and other long-term assistance;

(*h*)   To promote and establish effective instruments of co-operation in the fields of industry, science and technology, transport, shipping and mass communication media.

2. Developed countries should support initiatives in the regional, subregional and interregional co-operation of developing countries through

the extension of financial and technical assistance by more effective and concrete actions, particularly in the field of commercial policy.

VIII.   ASSISTANCE IN THE EXERCISE OF PERMANENT SOVEREIGNTY
OF STATES OVER NATURAL RESOURCES

All efforts should be made:

(*a*)   To defeat attempts to prevent the free and effective exercise of the rights of every State to full and permanent sovereignty over its natural resources;

(*b*)   To ensure that competent agencies of the United Nations system meet requests for assistance from developing countries in connexion with the operation of nationalized means of production.

IX.   STRENGTHENING THE ROLE OF THE UNITED NATIONS SYSTEM
IN THE FIELD OF INTERNATIONAL ECONOMIC CO-OPERATION

1. In furtherance of the objectives of the International Development Strategy for the Second United Nations Development Decade and in accordance with the aims and objectives of the Declaration on the Establishment of a New International Economic Order, all Member States pledge to make full use of the United Nations system in the implementation of the present Programme of Action, jointly adopted by them, in working for the establishment of a new international economic order and thereby strengthening the role of the United Nations in the field of worldwide co-operation for economic and social development.

2. The General Assembly of the United Nations shall conduct an overall review of the implementation of the Programme of Action as a priority item. All the activities of the United Nations system to be undertaken under the Programme of Action as well as those already planned, such as the World Population Conference, 1974, the World Food Conference, the Second General Conference of the United Nations Industrial Development Organization and the mid-term review and appraisal of the International Development Strategy for the Second United Nations Development Decade should be so directed as to enable the special session of the General Assembly on development, called for under Assembly resolution 3172 (XXVIII) of 17 December 1973, to make its full contribution to the establishment of the new international economic order. All Member States are urged, jointly and individually, to direct their efforts and policies towards the success of that special session.

3. The Economic and Social Council shall define the policy framework and co-ordinate the activities of all organizations, institutions and subsidiary bodies within the United Nations system which shall be entrusted with the task of implementing the present Programme of Action. In order

ro enable the Economic and Social Council to carry out its tasks effectively:

(*a*) All organizations, institutions and subsidiary bodies concerned within the United Nations system shall submit to the Economic and Social Council progress reports on the implementation of the Programme of Action within their respective fields of competence as often as necessary, but not less than once a year;

(*b*) The Economic and Social Council shall examine the progress reports as a matter or urgency, to which end it may be convened, as necessary, in special session or, if need be, may function continuously. It shall draw the attention of the General Assembly to the problems and difficulties arising in connexion with the implementation of the Programme of Action.

4. All organizations, institutions, subsidiary bodies and conferences of the United Nations system are entrusted with the implementation of the Programme of Action. The activities of the United Nations Conference on Trade and Development, as set forth in General Assembly resolution 1995 (XIX) of 30 December 1964, should be strengthened for the purpose of following in collaboration with other competent organizations the development of international trade in raw materials throughout the world.

5. Urgent and effective measures should be taken to review the lending policies of international financial institutions, taking into account the special situation of each developing country, to suit urgent needs, to improve the practices of these institutions in regard to, *inter alia*, development financing and international monetary problems, and to ensure more effective participation by developing countries — whether recipients or contributors — in the decision-making process through appropriate revision of the pattern of voting rights.

6. The developed countries and others in a position to do so should contribute substantially to the various organizations, programmes and funds established within the United Nations system for the purpose of accelerating economic and social development in developing countries.

7. The present Programme of Action complements and strengthens the goals and objectives embodied in the International Development Strategy for the Second United Nations Development Decade as well as the new measures formulated by the General Assembly at its twenty-eighth session to offset the shortfalls in achieving these goals and objectives.

8. The implementation of the Programme of Action should be taken into account at the time of the mid-term review and appraisal of the International Development Strategy for the Second United Nations Development Decade. New commitments, changes, additions and adaptations in

the Strategy should be made, as appropriate, taking into account the Declaration on the Establishment of a New International Economic Order and the present Programme of Action.

X.   SPECIAL PROGRAMME

The General Assembly adopts the following Special Programme, including particularly emergency measures to mitigate the difficulties of the developing countries most seriously affected by economic crisis, bearing in mind the particular problem of the least developed and land-locked countries:

The General Assembly,

Taking into account the following considerations:

(*a*)   The sharp increase in the prices of their essential imports such as food, fertilizers, energy products, capital goods, equipment and services, including transportation and transit costs, has gravely exacerbated the increasingly adverse terms of trade of a number of developing countries, added to the burden of their foreign debt and, cumulatively, created a situation which, if left untended, will make it impossible for them to finance their essential imports and development and result in a further deterioration in the levels and conditions of life in these countries. The present crisis is the outcome of all the problems that have accumulated over the years: in the field of trade, in monetary reform, the world-wide inflationary situation, inadequacy and delay in provision of financial assistance and many other similar problems in the economic and developmental fields. In facing the crisis, this complex situation must be borne in mind so as to ensure that the Special Programme adopted by the international community provides emergency relief and timely assistance to the most seriously affected countries. Simultaneously, steps are being taken to resolve these outstanding problems through a fundamental restructuring of the world economic system, in order to allow these countries while solving the present difficulties to reach an acceptable level of development.

(*b*)   The special measures adopted to assist the most seriously affected countries must encompass not only the relief which they require on an emergency basis to maintain their import requirements, but also, beyond that, steps to consciously promote the capacity of these countries to produce and earn more. Unless such a comprehensive approach is adopted, there is every likelihood that the difficulties of the most seriously affected countries may be perpetuated. Nevertheless, the first and most pressing task of the international community is to enable these countries to meet the shortfall in their balance-of-payments positions. But this must be simultaneously supplemented by additional development assistance to maintain and thereafter accelerate their rate of economic development.

(*c*)   The countries which have been most seriously affected are precisely those which are at the greatest disadvantage in the world economy: the least developed, the land-locked and other low-income developing countries as well as other developing countries whose economies have been seriously dislocated as a result of the present economic crisis, natural calamities, and foreign aggression and occupation. An indication of the countries thus affected the level of the impact on their economies and the kind of relief and assistance they require can be assessed on the basis, *inter alia*, of the following criteria:

(i)   Low *per capita* income as a reflection of relative poverty, low productivity, low level of technology and development;

(ii)   Sharp increase in their import cost of essentials relative to export earnings;

(iii) High ratio of debt servicing to export earnings;

(iv) Insufficiency in export earnings, comparative inelasticity of export incomes and unavailability of exportable surplus;

(v)   Low level of foreign exchange reserves or their inadequacy for requirements;

(vi) Adverse impact of higher transportation and transit costs;

(vii) Relative importance of foreign trade in the development process.

(*d*)   The assessment of the extent and nature of the impact on the economies of the most seriously affected countries must be made flexible, keeping in mind the present uncertainty in the world economy, the adjustment policies that may be adopted by the developed countries and the flow of capital and investment. Estimates of the payments situation and needs of these countries can be assessed and projected reliably only on the basis of their average performance over a number of years. Long term projections, at this time, cannot but be uncertain.

(*e*)   It is important that, in the special measures to mitigate the difficulties of the most seriously affected countries, all the developed countries as well as the developing countries should contribute according to their level of development and the capacity and strength of their economies. It is notable that some developing countries, despite their own difficulties and development needs, have shown a willingness to play a concrete and helpful role in ameliorating the difficulties faced by the poorer developing countries. The various initiatives and measures taken recently by certain developing countries with adequate resources on a bilateral and multilateral basis to contribute to alleviating the difficulties of other developing countries are a reflection of their commitment to the principle of effective economic co-operation among developing countries.

(*f*)   The response of the developed countries which have by far the greater capacity to assist the affected countries in overcoming their present difficulties must be commensurate with their responsibilities. Their assistance should be in addition to the presently available levels of aid. They should fulfil and if possible exceed the targets of the International Development Strategy for the Second United Nations Development Decade on financial assistance to the developing countries, especially that relating to official development assistance. They should also give serious consideration to the cancellation of the external debts of the most seriously affected countries. This would provide the simplest and quickest relief to the affected countries. Favourable consideration should also be given to debt moratorium and rescheduling. The current situation should not lead to industrialized countries to adopt what will ultimately prove to be a self-defeating policy aggravating the present crisis.

Recalling the constructive proposals made by His Imperial Majesty the Shahanshah of Iran[8] and His Excellency Mr. Houari Boumediene, President of the People's Democratic Republic of Algeria,[9]

1. *Decides* to launch a Special Programme to provide emergency relief and development assistance to the developing countries most seriously affected, as a matter of urgency, and for the period of time necessary at least until the end of the Second United Nations Development Decade, to help them overcome their present difficulties and to achieve self-sustaining economic development;

2. *Decides* as a first step in the Special Programme to request the Secretary-General to launch an emergency operation to provide timely relief to the most seriously affected developing countries, as defined in subparagraph (*c*) above, with the aim of maintaining unimpaired essential imports for the duration of the coming twelve months and to invite the industrialized countries and other potential contributors to announce their contributions for emergency assistance, or intimate their intention to do so, by 15 June 1974 to be provided through bilateral or multilateral channels, taking into account the commitments and measures of assistance announced or already taken by some countries, and further requests the Secretary-General to report the progress of the emergency operation to the General Assembly at its twenty-ninth session, through the Economic and Social Council at its fifty-seventh session;

3. *Calls upon* the industrialized countries and other potential contributors to extend to the most seriously affected countries immediate relief

8. A/9548 annex.
9. *Official Records of the General Assembly, Sixth Special Session, Plenary Meetings*, 2208th meeting, paras 3–152.

and assistance which must be of an order of magnitude that is commensurate with the needs of these countries. Such assistance should be in addition to the existing level of aid and provided at a very early date to the maximum possible extent on a grant basis and, where not possible, on soft terms. The disbursement and relevant operational procedures and terms must reflect this exceptional situation. The assistance could be provided either through bilateral or multilateral channels, including such new institutions and facilities that have been or are to be set up. The special measures may include the following:

(*a*)   Special arrangements on particularly favourable terms and conditions including possible subsidies for and assured supplies of essential commodities and goods;

(*b*)   Deferred payments for all or part of imports of essential commodities and goods;

(*c*)   Commodity assistance, including food aid, on a grant basis or deferred payments in local currencies, bearing in mind that this should not adversely affect the exports of developing countries;

(*d*)   Long-term suppliers' credits on easy teams;

(*e*)   Long-term financial assistance on concessionary terms;

(*f*)   Drawings from special International Monetary Fund facilities on concessional terms;

(*g*)   Establishment of a link between the creation of special drawing rights and development assistance, taking into account the additional financial requirements of the most seriously affected countries;

(*h*)   Subsidies, provided bilaterally or multilaterally, for interest on funds available on commercial terms borrowed by the most seriously affected countries;

(*i*)   Debt renegotiation on a case-by-case basis with a view to concluding agreements on debt cancellation, moratorium or rescheduling;

(*j*)   Provision on more favourable terms of capital goods and technical assistance to accelerate the industrialization of the affected countries;

(*k*)   Investment in industrial and development projects on favourable terms;

(*l*)   Subsidizing the additional transit and transport costs, especially of the land-locked countries;

4. *Appeals* to the developed countries to consider favourably the cancellation, moratorium or rescheduling of the debts of the most seriously affected developing countries, on their request, as an important contribution to mitigating the grave and urgent difficulties of these countries;

5. *Decides* to establish a Special Fund under the auspices of the United Nations, through voluntary contributions from industrialized countries and other potential contributors, as a part of the Special Programme, to provide emergency relief and development assistance, which will commence its

operations at the latest by 1 January 1975;

6. *Establishes* an *Ad Hoc* Committee on the Special Programme, composed of thirty-six Member States appointed by the President of the General Assembly, after appropriate consultations, bearing in mind the purposes of the Special Fund and its terms of reference;

(*a*)   To make recommendations, *inter alia*, on the scope, machinery and modes of operation of the Special Fund, taking into account the need for:

(i)   Equitable representation on its governing body;

(ii)   Equitable distribution of its resources;

(iii)   Full utilization of the services and facilities of existing international organizations;

(iv)   The possibility of merging the United Nations Capital Development Fund with the operations of the Special Fund;

(v)   A central monitoring body to oversee the various measures being taken both bilaterally and multilaterally;

and, to this end, bearing in mind the different ideas and proposals submitted at the sixth special session, including those put forward by Iran[10] and those made at the 2208th plenary meeting, and the comments thereon, and the possibility of utilizing the Special Fund to provide an alternative channel for normal development assistance after the emergency period;

(*b*)   To monitor, pending commencement of the operations of the Special Fund, the various measures being taken both bilaterally and multilaterally to assist the most seriously affected countries;

(*c*)   To prepare, on the basis of information provided by the countries concerned and by appropriate agencies of the United Nations system, a broad assessment of:

(i)   The magnitude of the difficulties facing the most seriously affected countries;

(ii)   The kind and quantities of the commodities and goods essentially required by them;

(iii)   Their need for financial assistance;

(iv)   Their technical assistance requirements, including especially access to technology;

7. *Requests* the Secretary-General of the United Nations, the Secretary-General of the United Nations Conference on Trade and Development, the President of the International Bank for Reconstruction and Development, the Managing Director of the International Monetary Fund, the Administrator of the United Nations Development Programme and the heads of the other competent international organizations to assist the *Ad Hoc* Committee on the Special Programme in performing the functions

10. A/AC.166/L.15; see also A69548, annex.

assigned to it under paragraph 6 above, and to help, as appropriate, in the operations of the Special Fund;

8. *Requests* the International Monetary Fund to expedite decisions on:

(*a*)   The establishment of an extended special facility with a view to enabling the most seriously affected developing countries to participate in it on favourable terms;

(*b*)   The creation of special drawing rights and the early establishment of the link between their allocation and development financing;

(*c*)   The establishment and operation of the proposed new special facility to extend credits and subsidize interest charges on commercial funds borrowed by Member States, bearing in mind the interests of the developing countries and especially the additional financial requirements of the most seriously affected countries;

9. *Requests* the World Bank Group and the International Monetary Fund to place their managerial, financial and technical services at the disposal of Governments contributing to emergency financial relief so as to enable them to assist without delay in channelling funds to the recipients, making such institutional and procedural changes as may be required;

10.   *Invites* the United Nations Development Programme to take the necessary steps, particularly at the country level, to respond on an emergency basis to requests for additional assistance which it may be called upon to render within the framework of the Special Programme;

11.   *Requests* the *Ad Hoc* Committee on the Special Programme to submit its report and recommendations to the Economic and Social Council at its fifty-seventh session and invites the Council, on the basis of its consideration of that report, to submit suitable recommendations to the General Assembly at its twenty-ninth session;

12.   *Decides* to consider as a matter of high priority at its twenty-ninth session, within the framework of a new international economic order, the question of special measures for the most seriously affected countries.

2229th plenary meeting
1 May 1974

INDEX

abortion 24, 25
Accra 87
Acheson, Dean 37
Afghanistan 166
Africa 17, 18, 19, 20, 21, 23, 24, 25, 30,
    34, 52, 53, 54, 55, 60, 109
agriculture 17, 20, 49, 63, 67
    agricultural development 108
    agricultural production 95
    agricultural products 61, 75, 93, 101
    agricultural regulations 93
aid 59, 66, 78, 125, 147, 148, 149, 153,
    154, 168
    lend-lease aid 36
    lead lease deliveries 38
Algeria 52, 114
Algiers 96, 97, 98, 105
Amin, Samir 108
Amuzegar, Jahangir 124, 125
Andean Pact 171
Anglo Persian Oil Company 142
anti-trust legislation 100
Aquinas, Thomas 138
Argentina 17, 34, 55, 71, 111
Arusha 114
Asia 17, 18, 19, 20, 24, 25, 30, 33, 34,
    36, 54, 72, 128, 160
    Southern Asia 55
    Western Asia 55
Asian-African Conference in Bandung
    (1955) 87
astrologers 52
Atlantic 36
Atlantic Charter of (1941) 38, 75
Australia 17, 25, 27, 28, 29, 34, 92, 145
Austria 92, 112
automobile 49
automobile industry 31

Bairoch, Paul 57, 133, 134
balance of power 34
balance of payments 44, 50, 78, 148
balance of trade 26, 34, 55, 73, 78, 145
balanced federal budget 37
Bandung 87
    Bandung Conference 136
Bangladesh 26, 55
basic needs philosophy 156
Beim, David O 171
Belgium 21, 48, 133
    Belgian colonial authorities 53
Belgrade 88, 96
Benares 53
Berlin Conference (1884-85) 22
Bhagwati, Jagdish 128
Boer War 22
Boumedienne 97, 103
British Petroleum 100
Brandt Commission (Independent
    Commission on International
    Development Issues) 115
Brazil 17, 34, 71, 72, 140, 164, 170, 171
Brazzaville 52
Bretton Woods 41, 42, 43, 44
British Commonwealth 38
Bucharest 107
Buenos Aires 111
buffer stocks 110, 135, 138, 139, 140
Burma 31, 52, 55, 87
capital 21, 27, 29, 48, 69, 72, 89, 173
    capital earnings 36
    capital goods 60, 105
    capital inflow 28
    capital movements 124
    capitalism 16, 35, 58
    capitalist order *see* capitalist world
        order